Where
Do I Go
From Here?

Discovery
House
PUBLISHERS
BOX 3566 · GRAND RAPIDS, MI 49501

*PUBLISHING BOOKS THAT FEED
THE SOUL WITH THE WORD OF GOD.*

Where Do I Go From Here?

A Handbook for New Believers

Dave Branon

Library of Congress Cataloging-in-Publication Data

Branon, Dave.
    Where do I go from here? : a handbook for beginning
Christians / by Dave Branon
        p.   cm.

    ISBN 0–929239–80–6

    1. Converts—Religious life. 2. Christian life—1960–
3. Theology, Doctrinal—Popular works. I. Title.
BV4520.B643   1993
248.4—dc20   93–41779
                                                              CIP

Discovery House Publishers is affiliated with Radio Bible Class,
Grand Rapids, Michigan

Discovery House books are distributed to the trade by Thomas
Nelson Publishers, Nashville, Tennessee 37214

Printed in the United States of America

93 94 95 96 / CHG / 10 9 8 7 6 5 4 3 2 1

Contents

Introduction

She had never been to our church before. I knew that for certain.

A young woman. Maybe twenty-five years old. Black. And she sat next to my wife and me in our mostly white church that stands prominently in a changing neighborhood.

Although it is uncharacteristic of me to seek out and talk to visitors, I was eager to talk with her. I wanted more than anything to make her feel at home—to feel welcome. I wanted her to come back.

I noticed that when the missionary speaker that night asked us to turn to the book of Galatians in the Bible, she could not find it in her copy of the Scriptures. Afraid to offend her, yet sorry she couldn't locate the reading, I took the easy way out and did nothing. Maybe I should have helped her. Maybe not.

As soon as the final "Amen" was pronounced, I stuck out my hand, introduced myself, and began asking nosy questions.

What my wife and I found out as we talked with Pam was exciting. She had "found the Lord," as she called it, just a week or two earlier while watching a TV preacher. She couldn't recall the preacher's name, but she certainly seemed excited about what had happened in her life.

On this particular Sunday evening, as a new believer, she dressed up and headed for our church for one simple reason. It was close to her house.

"I just want to know more about the Lord," she said as we talked.

I knew that, although I hadn't been much help when she couldn't find Galatians, I wanted to help her now.

We took her name and address and noted her desire for a visit so our visitation pastor could call on her. And we handed her a copy of the devotional guide *Our Daily Bread.*

"This will help you by giving you something in the Bible to read every day," I explained.

As I thought about Pam and the many, many new Christians like her who are just beginning to grow accustomed to this new life of faith in Jesus Christ, I wondered if it wouldn't be helpful to them to have a beginner's handbook—a manual that could guide them through some of the key first things they need to know as new believers.

So, Pam, and everyone else trying to find Galatians and trying to understand all the other things that a lot of longtime Christians have discovered, this book is for you. It is one way we can say to you, "Welcome to the family."

Your decision to follow Jesus Christ and to commit your life to Him is great news! It not only assures you of a future home in heaven, but it also makes you a part of a rather remarkable, highly diverse family—a family of faith.

You now have brothers and sisters of all colors, shapes, and backgrounds all over the world—people who will welcome you into their lives any time you need their help. You have friends in your community who will love to meet you and help you grow in your faith.

As all of us do, you will run into times of loneliness, trouble, and disappointment. When you do, you won't have to struggle alone.

In the family of faith are people from all walks of life and from all levels of society who will listen to your cares and direct you to the help that can be found in our guidebook for living—God's Word, the Bible. And of course you always have the help of God Himself, who is listening for your prayer. If you needed love, you came to the right place when you came to Jesus.

We are a family of faith, and we want to help. This book is one attempt at giving you a positive entrance into the new life that stretches out before you. As a new believer, you are probably wondering where you are supposed to go from here. Perhaps you want to know how your faith in Jesus Christ will affect your life and your future. If so, this book may be just what you need to get your spiritual bearings and to get your life headed in the way God would have you go.

May the ideas and suggestions and facts you read here, along with the experiences you have in your new family of faith, help you find the true happiness, peace, joy, and hope that can be yours as you develop a close relationship with our Father through Jesus Christ.

1

An Incredible Rescue

What does it mean to be saved?

Everybody knows what it means to be saved. Physically, at least. We've all watched the evening news, spellbound, as people saved people.

Americans watched breathlessly several years ago as workers frantically carved a passageway out of rock to save tiny Jessica McClure. Stuck in a tiny well shaft, Jessica pictured for all of us what being saved represents. She was in a predicament that had only two alternatives: either someone would reach her and free her from her entrapment, or she would die. Without a rescue, she was doomed.

We saw it again during the Persian Gulf War when allied fliers were forced to parachute over enemy territory in Iraq. One downed airman in particular illustrates what salvation is about. United States helicopters sped through the air on their way to his rescue, while on the ground Iraqi trucks raced toward him. Which would get there first? Would he be saved or would he be doomed? Just minutes before the Iraqis would have had the airman in custody, the U.S. chopper sliced through the sky, fired on the incoming Iraqis, and swooped in for the rescue. It seemed that the airman's life hung in the balance as two forces—one representing his destruction and one representing his freedom—went after him.

Jessica McClure and that pilot were rescued. Snatched from danger. Given life.

They were saved. Physically saved.

But when we apply the words "saved" and "salvation" to the spiritual side of things, some people wonder what in the world we are talking about.

They hear preachers talk about being saved, and they get confused. They read about people—sometimes famous ones, like former White House aide Chuck Colson, or baseball pitcher Orel Hershiser—who have been saved, and they don't know how to respond. They wonder what they've been saved from. They question what good it does. They scoff at the suggestion that it is possible at all. Or even necessary.

Perhaps the skepticism and confusion are the result of the wide divergence of ideas about what it takes to be saved. Although none of Jessica's rescuers stood in that Midland, Texas, backyard and wondered what it would mean to save her, many people wonder just that about their souls. To save Jessica meant to get her out of a situation that would have led to her death. The same is true of us spiritually. We need something done that will get us out of a situation that, unless it changes, will lead to spiritual death.

Yet many people try to find salvation by doing things that just cannot get them out of harm's way.
- They follow a system of rules.
- They claim a belief in God.
- They try to do as many good works as they can.

- They try to follow the example set by Jesus in living a good life.
- They practice a religious ritual—like being baptized.

Think again of that American pilot trapped behind enemy lines in the Persian Gulf War. He was helpless. He was unable to do anything to secure his rescue. He could have followed all the rules in his Air Force training guide, but he still couldn't escape the Iraqis on his own. He could have chanted over and over that he believed in America. He could have folded his parachute up neatly and kept his shoes polished. It just didn't matter what he did. He was unable to save himself.

He could be saved only when someone else intervened and he accepted that offer to take him out of his precarious situation.

A couple of years ago, I asked the readers of *Campus Journal,* a daily devotional guide for young people, to tell me what they thought a Christian is. The answers for the most part revealed a good understanding of salvation and what it means to be saved. But there were some young people who had apparently not yet come to grips with the truth that to be saved means to be rescued from a situation over which we have absolutely no control. It seems that many of them think they must do something to get themselves saved. They forget that, like the trapped Jessica, they can do nothing to extricate themselves.

Here are some suggestions readers gave to explain what a Christian is.

- Someone who is trying hard to be like Jesus.
- Someone who wants to be Christlike.

• Someone who patterns his or her life after Jesus' example.

• Someone who makes a conscious effort to be a good person by using Jesus as an example.

• Someone who recognizes God as the Creator and holds the utmost fear and respect for Him, who loves Him and shares that love with others, and who is kind, generous, and forgiving.

• Someone who does his or her best to follow Christ as He is known in the Bible.

• Someone who believes in God.

• Someone who loves God and tries to do what He wants.

• Someone who is warm, friendly.

What admirable qualities! To be like Jesus. To be a good person. To recognize God as Creator. To be kind and generous. These are characteristics that make our mothers and schoolteachers happy and make life easier for everyone.

But they do not get us saved. These great qualities cannot begin to address the problem that every one of us faces: we are trapped by something we need to be saved from.

What we must be saved from is our unrighteous condition. Just as Jessica's well-shaft enclosure made it impossible for her to save herself, so our unrighteousness has us trapped. Look at how Paul, one of the people God used to write the Bible, described our situation. "There is no one righteous, not even one; there is no one who understands, no one who seeks God. All have turned away" (Romans 3:10–12). Later in that same chapter, Paul said, "All have sinned and fall short of the glory of God" (v. 23).

Each of us is trapped between heaven and hell in a perilous position. We are by nature unrighteous, or sinful, a condition that has condemned us to eternal death. We need someone to save us from a sure and certain spiritual demise.

While we hang there in the balance, fearful of facing the judgment of God because of our sin, we simply cannot free ourselves. But this is just what many people try to do. Let's look more closely at some man-made plans for salvation and see where they are flawed.

The follow-the-rules plan

Ironically, this is, in the original design, the right plan. We can see it in the Bible in Genesis 1. Adam and Eve in the Garden of Eden could have maintained their right relationship with God by obeying one basic rule: Don't eat from the tree of the knowledge of good and evil. But Satan talked them right out of perfection and eternal glory by convincing them that God didn't know what He was talking about.

That took care of the rest of us, because Adam and Eve as our original parents passed their sinful nature on down the line. This placed us all in the unenviable situation of being condemned to spiritual death—unless someone rescues us. Here's how Paul described it in Romans 5:12: "Therefore, just as sin entered the world through one man, and death through sin, . . . in this way death came to all men, because all sinned."

Once humankind had been stamped permanently with the label "sinful," perfection was no longer attainable. No one could achieve the desired goal

of fellowship with God. No one could be worthy to enter God's glory. The follow-the-rules plan was no
longer in effect.

That hasn't stopped people from trying it,
though. One group who tried a self-salvation scheme
were called Pharisees. They lived in Israel at the
same time Jesus did—about two thousand years
ago. They knew they needed some kind of salvation;
it was indelibly etched in their consciousness
through their vast knowledge of Jewish history.

So they set about to develop a plan. If motives
count, it was an admirable plan. They wanted to
please God by setting up a system of standards by
which they should live. Even their name, which
means "separated ones," implies that they wanted to
stay away from evil. According to their plan, they were
to pay ten percent of their income to the temple, maintain ceremonial purity in following the Jewish religious rituals, and follow the smallest details of their
traditions. Over the years, they came up with hundreds of regulations to follow. Even the apostle Paul,
a former Pharisee himself, seemed to be impressed
with their faithfulness to the law (Philippians 3:5).

The Pharisees' plan to bring themselves to God
included many good things, but it could not get
them rescued. Matthew 23 records how Jesus took
apart their platform for getting to God, plank by
plank. Although He recognized their external goodness (v. 25), He condemned the results of all they
had done. In all their efforts, Jesus made clear, the
Pharisees had not discovered the way of salvation.

Thus it always will be with anyone who hopes to
rescue himself by following a set of rules. There is no
such thing as a do-it-yourself kit for being saved.

The good works plan

Suppose you were a school teacher. High school. Algebra. You had a student who was about the nicest person you could ask for. Polite to everyone. Never any trouble. Except when it came to algebra. This student simply refused to do things your way. For some reason, this student would not do the problems assigned in the way they were assigned. His papers were always neat and orderly, but instead of using the formula you taught, he worked by trial and error, with a heavy tendency toward the error part.

Consequently this student never got any problems right. As a result he got no credit for homework and always failed the tests. Even when you gave him personal attention to explain things, he wouldn't change.

But that didn't discourage this student. He was making a career out of extra credit. He would wash your chalkboard, empty the trash cans, and sweep the floor for you. He would do pages and pages of math problems and hand them in (but never algebra problems). He was the most tireless worker you ever saw.

Yet when it came time to hand out the grades, what could you do but fail this student? All the extra work may have been helpful to you, but it did nothing to change his grade. Other than the built-in value that doing any good thing has for the person who does it, the student's work was worthless. It had no value in relationship to his score as a student in your class.

What many people try to do with God is what that fictitious student tried to do in your imaginary class. Far from trying the follow-the-rules plan, they ignore even the instructions God has clearly given as to how they can "pass the course." Instead of doing what He said to do, they create their own curriculum and try to grade themselves on what they have done. They pass Being Kind 101 with flying colors. They ace their self-created class called Help the Needy. They breeze through, never stopping to consider that they are getting no credit for their efforts. Extra credit, they forget, comes only after a student has first fulfilled the basic requirements.

Let's go to the Bible—to Romans 4—to see what Paul said about this matter of works. To illustrate his teaching on faith and works, Paul dug back into Old Testament history and dusted off the story of a man named Abraham. Abraham would be a first-ballot inductee into the Works Hall of Fame. He showed selflessness by allowing his nephew Lot to take the best land (see Genesis 13). He showed courage by rescuing Lot from the band of kings who captured him (see Genesis 14). And he showed compassion by pleading for God to spare Lot from the destruction of Sodom and Gomorrah (see Genesis 18 and 19). If God wanted something done, Abraham was the man to do it for Him.

Yet look at Romans 4:2. It says, "If, in fact, Abraham was justified by works, he had something to boast about—but not before God." Paul was making it clear that, as impressed as we are with what Abraham did, it could not gain favor with God. There was something else that had to come first. That something is faith.

"Abraham believed God," Paul explains in verse 3, "and it was credited to him as righteousness."

Clearly, Abraham's belief—his faith—gained him the righteousness that only God can give.

Just as a teacher can accept extra credit only after a student has fulfilled the requirements for the course, so can God accept our extra credit works only after we fulfill the requirement of faith. Notice Paul's explanation. "The words 'it was credited to him' were written not for him alone, but also for us, to whom God will credit righteousness—for us who believe in Him who raised Jesus Christ from the dead" (Romans 4:23–24). Only by faith in Jesus Christ and His sacrifice can we gain favor with God.

The belief-in-God plan

It almost doesn't seem fair that the belief-in-God method doesn't work. After all, isn't that what the Bible is all about—telling us about God? If we believe that He exists, shouldn't that give us a one-way ticket to heaven?

It would certainly be comforting to think that way. According to some estimates, only about 5 percent of the world's population are atheists. That would mean that 95 percent of the five billion people in the world believe in God, or at least are willing to admit the possibility that He exists.

Sound surprising? Look at it from the other side: actually, the surprise in those statistics is that 5 percent of the world's population does not admit to a belief in God. According to Romans 1:18–20, God's existence is plainly revealed in His world for all to see. Those who say they do not believe in God have willfully rejected that knowledge. They "suppress the truth by their wickedness," as Paul put it (1:18). Belief in God, Paul said, is no remarkable achievement—and surely not the sole criterion for salvation. Salvation involves something deeper, something more profound than simple acknowledgment of God's existence.

Another Bible writer who made it clear that simple belief in God is not enough is James. He wrote this: "You believe that there is one God. Good! Even the demons believe that—and shudder" (James 2:19). No, belief in God, as good as it is, is not enough to rescue our souls from spiritual death.

On the surface, you may sense a discrepancy between the fact that Abraham was credited with righteousness because of his belief, while James tells us that to believe is not enough. There is a difference, though, between believing in God and believing God. We are told in Genesis 15:6 and Romans 4:3 that Abraham "believed God," which means he trusted Him and was willing to place his life in God's hands. Galatians 3 clarifies this idea further. After reiterating the idea that Abraham "believed God, and it was credited to him as righteousness," Paul equated his belief with the term *faith*. He said, "Those who have faith are blessed along with Abraham, the man of faith" (3:9). Abraham did not just believe that God exists, he entrusted his life to Him. Therein lies the difference.

The live-like-Jesus plan

Have you ever observed someone you really admire and then said to yourself, "I wish I could do things like that"? Maybe this person always seems to have a toothpaste commercial smile and the pleasant look of someone who just got a raise. So you decide that tomorrow you're going to be that way.

But the traffic is heavy, the car is making that clanking noise again, your boss meets you at the door with extra work, and you have a headache. Despite your desire to be as vibrant and friendly as the person you admire, you can't do it. Even on a good day you just can't seem to be that other person.

It is easy to look around at others and see how you would like to change. More hair. Less weight. More wit. Less anxiety. But even when we try to emulate that person who seems to have it all, we always seem to fail, to fall short.

We are not that other person. Our traits and his or her traits are different, and we cannot will them into existence in our lives.

Perhaps you can see the direction I'm taking.

There once lived a Man who became the world's best role model. He was compassionate, thoughtful, strong, peaceful, intelligent, and humble. When we look at Him, we can't help but want to follow His example, to be like Him. And we are welcome to try to do so.

The New Testament tells us that we should follow Jesus' example. Here's how Peter put it: "Christ suffered for you, leaving you an example, that you should follow in his steps" (1 Peter 2:21).

The apostle Paul also thought it was a good idea to try to live like Jesus. He wrote, "Follow my example, as I follow the example of Christ" (1 Corinthians 11:1). Yes, we are clearly told that we should try to be like Jesus.

But we cannot be like Him in the most important way. Try as we might, we cannot be perfect, sinless, and God. These words all describe Jesus in a way that we can never even hope to be described. As

much as we admire those characteristics of Jesus,
we can't possess them.

We are flawed; He is perfect.

We sin; He is sinless.

We are mortal humans; He is the God-man.

Our nature will not allow us to be enough like
Jesus to be made acceptable to God. No matter how
hard we try. We could travel to the farthest reaches
of the world in Jesus' name. We could work to eliminate poverty. We could feed hungry children. We
could give humanitarian aid to the poorest people in
our town. We could do all that and not gain entrance
into God's family. Our sinfulness would always de-
tain us.

A live-like-Jesus plan will never work. It might
make us feel better. It might help the people we are
assisting. It might do a lot of good things. But it will
never erase the fact that we need to be rescued from
impending spiritual death. That rescue will come
only when God forgives us our sin through the mer-
its of what Jesus did for us in dying on the cross.
Our faith in Jesus Christ is how we show that we realize our need and are willing to receive the rescue
He offers.

The religious ritual plan
Baptism. Communion. Lighting candles. Praying to-
ward Mecca. Visiting shrines. Taking pilgrimages.
Studying a catechism. Climbing steps. Reenacting
Bible scenes.

The list could go on and on. There are religious
rituals for everything. Some are good. Some are
worthless.

Some come out of biblical history. Some are historical traditions. Some come from churches. Some from literature.

But none lead to salvation.

None.

There's a certain irony to this fact. The irony is that in the Old Testament of the Bible the religious ritual plan was the way to go.

The Old Testament books of Exodus and Leviticus are full of rituals. The people had to wash this and burn that. They had to pick out the unblemished animals and spread blood on the right locations. It was hard to keep up with all the details.

Perhaps the greatest ritual was the original Passover. According to Exodus 12, this ritual wasn't a matter of religion; it was a matter of life and death. Each family that followed the rules for the ritual— which included taking a year-old, perfect male lamb, slaughtering it at twilight, putting some of its blood on the doorframes of the house, and then cooking and eating the lamb—would not have their firstborn killed. Now that's a ritual that would get your attention!

Another ritual that had unquestionable value to the Israelites was what went on inside the tabernacle during the forty years they wandered through the wilderness. Here again exacting details were given, and the priests had to perform their services correctly.

In the Old Testament, salvation indeed included ritual.

But that all changed when Jesus died on the cross. When He died, the curtain of the temple split in two (Matthew 27:51), which meant that the old method of coming to God, through priests and rituals, was no longer valid. Now a more direct route was open.

Hebrews 10 talks about it. "It is impossible," the author wrote, "for the blood of bulls and goats to take away sins" (10:4). Those sacrificial rituals of the Old Testament, which represented temporary answers to the sin problem, were replaced in the New Testament by a divine sacrifice. "We have been made holy," the passage goes on, "through the sacrifice of the body of Jesus Christ once for all" (10:10).

As Jesus died He proclaimed, "It is finished" (John 19:30). His work of providing salvation was done. Anything we do to attempt to gain salvation through ritual is empty, meaningless activity when compared with Jesus' ultimate sacrifice.

All religions have their rituals. Many are done carefully, reverently, and in an attitude of worship. But none of them accomplish the work Jesus did for us when "he saved us, not because of righteous things we had done, but because of his mercy" (Titus 3:5).

The only plan that works

People who are in danger—real danger—must depend on their rescuers. A drowning swimmer must trust the lifeguard or sink to the bottom. A choking restaurant patron must depend on the strong arms of someone who knows the Heimlich maneuver or run out of air. It's simple logic that those on the brink cannot pull themselves back from the edge. They need intervention.

And so it is with spiritual life. Each of us stands on the brink, helplessly teetering on the edge of eternal separation from God. By nature, we stand condemned—doomed to a sure spiritual death if something isn't done. But next to us, ready to snatch us from the fate that awaits us, stands Jesus. Patiently He waits for us to let Him rescue us. He doesn't want us to fall; in fact Peter said that "he is patient with you, not wanting anyone to perish, but everyone to come to repentance" (2 Peter 3:9). He Himself said it like this: "For God did not send his Son into the world to condemn the world, but to save the world through him" (John 3:17).

There's the picture. Like a lifeguard poised to jump into the water and bring the struggling swimmer out of the deadly surf, so Jesus waits for us to call on Him in faith so He can rescue us.

Have you let Him do that for you? Have you recognized that you cannot save yourself through following rules, trying to pile up good works, claiming to believe in God, following Jesus' good example, or doing something religious? Have you realized that because of your sin you are as helpless as a baby trapped in a well shaft, and that the only way you can get rescued is to put your faith in Jesus' ability to save you because of His sacrificial death on the cross? If you have put your faith in Jesus to rescue you, then you know what it means to be saved. You've experienced an incredible rescue.

Getting into the Word

Using your Bible, look up each of these verses and summarize what each passage tells you about salvation.

- Luke 19:10
- John 3:14–17
- John 4:14

- John 12:47
- Acts 4:12
- Acts 11:17–18
- Acts 16:17, 30–31
- Romans 1:5, 16–17
- Romans 5:1–2
- 2 Corinthians 5:17, 21
- Galatians 2:16

Thinking it through

Consider the following questions as you reflect on what you have read in this chapter.

- Why do so many people seek God in ways that are so much more complicated than the simple gospel?
- What were some of the obstacles you had in accepting the truth that the gospel was really the way to God?
- What convinced you that Christ was indeed the only way?
- What verses in the Bible were especially helpful to you as you began to understand the truth of salvation? Why did those verses help you so much?
- What has your salvation rescued you from?
- Whom do you know who can help you go from taking your first baby steps, to walking, to running as a Christian?

Getting practical

Try these suggestions for applying what you have read.

- Write out your salvation testimony in fifty to a hundred words.

• Tell two people about your new faith in Jesus Christ.

• Record what happened when you told them and what you learned during the conversations.

Exploring the subject further

If you'd like to read more about the one way to salvation, any of these books is a good place to start.

• *Mere Christianity*, C.S. Lewis

• *Our Sufficiency in Christ*, John F. MacArthur

• *Born Again*, Charles Colson

2

An Exciting New Name

What does it mean to be called a Christian?

Have you ever listened to parents-to-be as they talk about what to name the baby? They feel joy mixed with anxiety, stirred up with "helpful" advice offered by everybody from the prospective grandparents on down to the clerk at the grocery store. The new mom and dad get only one chance to stick a label on their infant, and they want to get it right.

They know that the handle they hang on their baby will affect him or her throughout life. People who study such things even contend that certain names contribute to the personality of the child as he or she grows up. Supposedly there are names that you give your child if you want him to be a football player (Bruno, perhaps) or if you want him to be a piano player (Wolfgang, maybe).

Your name is a most special possession. No other sound is quite as nice as hearing someone call your name (unless of course you hear it from a police officer who is looking at your license and saying, "Well, Sandy Jones, do you always drive 55 in a 25 mph zone?").

Names are important to God, too. In fact, He went so far as to change the names of several Bible people, because it makes a difference to Him what we are called. He renamed Abram, for instance, calling him Abraham. And Sarai, Abraham's wife, became Sarah.

But the most important indication of God's interest in names comes in the New Testament, in the story of the One coming to redeem the world.

Jesus—not just a first name

Read what happened after Mary received word from an angel that she would be the mother of the "Son of God," as the announcing messenger called Him (Luke 1:35). Joseph, to whom Mary was pledged to be married, was also visited by an angel, who had a specific message about what to name the baby. Joseph was told, "You are to give him the name Jesus, because he will save his people from their sins" (Matthew 1:21).

The name *Jesus,* even though it was a name other boys in that culture were given, was significant because it means "Yahweh [or God] saves." In that name lies everything that is most vital about this baby's arrival on earth through a human mother. To call Him Jesus meant to spell out clearly the work He came to do. He was not Jesus because He was going to be a good role model or because He would teach people how to suffer. No, He was called Jesus "because he will save his people from their sins." God wanted Joseph to give Mary's little Lamb this name because it showed Jesus for what He came to be—a Savior.

Christ—not Jesus' last name

There's a second name we often use to identify our Savior, and this part of His name is the one that you will be hearing attached to your name now that you have become a follower of Jesus. The New Testament tells us that this Jesus—the one born to Mary in a Bethlehem manger—is the Christ. Or, as we commonly refer to Him, Jesus Christ.

The name *Christ* isn't Jesus' last name. It's a title, like president or prime minister. This second designation made it clear to the people in Jesus' day that He was the *Messiah,* the Hebrew equivalent of that important title. It means simply, "the anointed one." To those people this dual name of Jesus, the One who would save, and Christ, God's Anointed, was the indication they needed that this Man was no ordinary person.

Christian—our family name

It was quite a while, however, before anybody who followed Jesus Christ took on His name as we do. According to the book of Acts, which records events that happened after Jesus died, rose from the grave, and ascended into heaven, the disciples of Jesus were first called *Christians* while they were visiting the town of Antioch (11:26).

We don't know whether they chose this name for themselves or whether someone else foisted it on them as a slander, but it stuck. And even if it was meant to be demeaning at first, it was appropriate. It means, literally, "an adherent of Christ."

Two other times in the New Testament the word *Christian* is used. Perhaps fifteen years after the name was first used at Antioch, the Roman king

Agrippa talked with the apostle Paul about the new faith that was spreading throughout the lands around the Mediterranean Sea. After listening to Paul's explanation of the faith and after discussing it with him, Agrippa said to Paul, "Do you think that in such a short time you can persuade me to be a Christian?" (Acts 26:28). The term must have been in common use at this time, and King Agrippa knew the significance of it.

His reaction to Paul's evangelistic outreach shows us that adopting the name "Christian" is not a flippant matter. Agrippa apparently was not prompted by the Holy Spirit of God to become a Christian, but even Agrippa, in his unbelief, knew that this was a matter of utmost importance. When a person puts his or her faith in Christ, it's not an action to be taken lightly.

In a later New Testament book, 1 Peter, the name *Christian* is used for the third time in the Bible. Here we see still another view of what it means for us to carry the name around with us: it might mean trouble.

"Do not be surprised," Peter wrote, "at the painful trial you are suffering" (1 Peter 4:12). Bearing this new name, he said, could make things rough for you. But Peter also gave clear assurances that blessings and glory await those who not only wear Jesus' name as "Christians" but who also rejoice that they can "participate in the sufferings of Christ" (4:13). "If you suffer as a Christian, do not be ashamed, but praise God that you bear that name" (4:16).

No matter what troubles it might cause for us to have a name that lets people know we follow Christ the Savior and Messiah, we are still far better off than anybody who does not carry that name. We can praise God because as bearers of the name *Christian* we have so much going for us.

Let's take a look at your new family name two different ways. First, let's see what it doesn't mean to carry the name *Christian,* and second, let's examine what it does mean.

What the name Christian is not

Not a name that means anything by itself without faith. The title alone does not save us. Jesus said that there will be people who will call on Him, thinking they are ready to go into His kingdom, but they will be left outside. The name *Christian* refers to people who are followers of Jesus. To put that label on a person who does not have faith in Jesus Christ is to misname that person. "And without faith," the author of Hebrews wrote, "it is impossible to please God" (11:6).

When I taught school, I noticed that students occasionally decided they didn't like their names anymore. One day a girl preferred the name Elizabeth, and the next day she preferred Liz. Nothing about her was changed. For some reason she just felt better about herself with that new name. But she wasn't any different merely because she gave herself a new name.

A few years later, though, after Elizabeth finished school, I saw her again. By then her name really *was* changed—her last name. She was married, and her new last name represented a significant change in her life. She was a member of a new family.

Just as that student could pretend to have a new name and have nothing change in her life, so we

could pretend to take on the name Christian (as
many people do) but have it not affect our lives at all.
Only when we put our faith in Jesus Christ and thus
become members of His family can we rightfully
wear His family name, Christian.

Not a magic word that makes all problems disappear.
We'll get into this subject in more detail in a later
chapter, but you need to understand up front that
being a Christian will not solve all of your problems.

A look at the life of Paul (one of the Bible writers
and a person we will be referring to quite often in
this book) spells that out clearly. Before Paul put his
faith in Jesus Christ, he was a powerful religious
leader. He was a Jew who took pride in his ability to
beat up Christians. As a Pharisee, he thought it was
his duty to try to wipe out this new faith through ter-
rorist tactics. He was almost like a first-century Ma-
fia don who had great power at his disposal and
nothing to hold him back from his mission. He
caused all kinds of trouble for people who believed in
Jesus, but at this stage in his life he himself probably led a rather trouble-free existence.

Then he became a Christian (read about it in
Acts 9). That's when his difficulties started. As the
man who was one of Jesus' greatest apostles of all
time, you might think Paul deserved a life of ease,
perhaps spending the weekends on his yacht in the
Mediterranean. After all, he was a sincere man of
faith who worked hard to spread the gospel.
Shouldn't he be rewarded with a painless existence?

Check out some of the details:
    • "Day and night [the Jews] kept close watch on
    the city gates in order to kill him. But his follow-

ers took him by night and lowered him in a basket through an opening in the wall" (Acts 9:24–25).

• "They stoned Paul and dragged him outside the city, thinking he was dead" (Acts 14:19).

• "The crowd joined in the attack against Paul and Silas, and the magistrates ordered them to be stripped and beaten. After they had been severely flogged, they were thrown into prison" (Acts 16:22–23).

• "Five times I received from the Jews the forty lashes minus one. Three times I was beaten with rods, once I was stoned, three times I was shipwrecked, . . . I have known hunger and thirst and have often gone without food; I have been cold and naked" (2 Corinthians 11:24–25, 27).

Paul did not wear the name *Christian* as a shield to deflect problems. It was more like a homing device that attracted them, because his excitement for telling others how Jesus Christ had changed his life and could change theirs, too, put him at odds with people wherever he went. Yet it was a price he was willing to pay. He bore the name with honor.

Not an indication of weakness or lack of intelligence. If you believe what you see in the popular media, all preachers are Barney Fife-types and all Christians are ignorant hypocrites with no backbone. Perhaps you have seen Christians characterized that way on television programs or in movies.

Whatever reasons the producers have for making the name *Christian* appear to be a label of weakness, they can't make the label stick. Such a characterization ignores people like Olympic decathlon athlete Dave Johnson, and 1988 Cy Young and World Series MVP Orel Hershiser, and 1991 Super Bowl-winning quarterback Jeff Hostetler, and Olympic wrestling gold medalist Ben Peterson, and NBA All-Star David Robinson, and pro golfing champion Betsy King. These people have a strong faith in Jesus Christ while showing how to maintain strength, determination, endurance, and whatever it takes to win, fair and square. There's nothing weak about these Christians.

And just as becoming a person of faith does not mean we become weak, neither does it mean we check our brains at the door. Society can boast an impressive list of top thinkers who proudly wear the name Christian. Many United States presidents have openly declared their faith, including most of those in recent memory. Top policy makers of the past several years, such as former surgeon general Dr. C. Everett Koop and former secretary of state James Baker, were not afraid to be called Christians. World-renowned neurosurgeon Ben Carlson is a man of faith.

Christianity is a thinking person's faith. It makes sense because it is a reasonable, logical extension of history. Christianity alone offers the answer to life's tough questions, and it alone offers the power to make the weak strong.

Not an isolationist term. If you have just recently become a child of God by accepting Jesus' gift of faith, you may have an occasional urge to keep the news from people. Despite your enthusiasm for what Christ has done for you by saving you, you may grow timid when approached about your faith. You may wish to run and hide and not have to explain it to anybody. Perhaps it is too personal to tell someone else.

The Bible, the guideline for Christian living, has a message for us about that. We aren't supposed to tramp off to some cave somewhere and keep the good news to ourselves. Instead, we are told to go into the world and tell other people what we have found—that Jesus saves (Mark 16:15). It is our distinct honor, privilege, and responsibility to tell other people about Christ.

Think about the fact that the Christian faith has been passed down from generation to generation to generation for almost two thousand years. Although there have been great evangelists and preachers who spread the gospel to thousands at a time, most of the progress of Christianity has happened as one person told another, who told another.

During the first couple hundred years after Jesus died, rose, and ascended into heaven, the Christian church spread mostly by word of mouth throughout the Mediterranean Sea area and what is now southern Europe. Non-Christians lived next to and observed Christians and saw that they lived better, more moral, more honorable lives—sometimes in spite of severe persecution.

We can spread the message the same way today, no matter how new we are in the faith. But we can't do it if we are isolationists.

We've seen a few things the name Christian is not. Perhaps that has given us some courage to challenge those who really do not understand what this name means.

What the name Christian is

A name that identifies us with the pivotal person in history. You don't have to search long to realize that Jesus is a key figure in history. One solid proof of that is in our designation of years on the calendar. Historians long ago divided history into two parts: B.C. and A.D. B.C. means "before Christ," and AD means "anno Domini," which is Latin for "in the year of our Lord." Without realizing it, each person who refers to a calendar or writes the date on a check or a letter is paying homage to the central figure in history.

Yet Jesus as a key figure in history is different from Jesus as the Savior. In other words, when we attach ourselves to the name *Christian,* we are doing something that goes far beyond recognizing an important historical person. When we call ourselves "Christians," we tell everyone that we know Jesus is still alive, is in heaven with God the Father, and hears us, cares for us, and answers our prayers. When we take on the name *Christian,* we are identifying ourselves as members of a unique group—a group that believes not only that Jesus existed in history but also that He is alive two thousand years later and can make a difference in our lives.

Not everyone will applaud us for that kind of devotion—even to the pivotal person in history.

A name that may divide people. Jesus warned us this would happen. "Do you think I came to bring peace on earth?" He asked. "No, I tell you, but division. From now on there will be five in one family divided against each other, three against two and two against three" (Luke 12:51). These words of the Savior take a bit of explaining, for some say that they contradict what we normally think about Jesus.

Even before you became a Christian, you probably heard people talking at Christmastime about "Peace on earth, good will toward men." That was the message a band of angels brought to a motley group of shepherds who soon trekked to Bethlehem to worship the baby Jesus. Those angels were talking about the peace that you experienced when you accepted Jesus as your Savior. You experienced peace with God—which we can have only through Jesus.

Now, peace with people and peace with God are two different things. When Jesus said that He brought division, not peace, He was saying that there would be divisions when one person in a family became a follower of His and another person in the family did not. In other words, salvation promises rescue from eternal separation from God and it gives peace with God, but it cannot guarantee peace with people. There are no guarantees that family members will always openly and enthusiastically accept the news that a person in the family has become a Christian.

This may happen to you. Because of your faith, you may face the angry words and sharp criticism of friends or loved ones. You may wonder if it is worth the hassle.

It is.

It may sound like trouble is definitely coming, but it doesn't have to be that way. There are many verses in the New Testament that can encourage you when you fear that conflicts are on the horizon. Your reaction to others and your example of Christian testimony can head off many potential problems.

Here are some verses that can help you extend the peace you have with God to your relationships with others.

• "If it is possible, as far as it depends on you, live at peace with everyone" (Romans 12:18). The passage goes on to tell how it can be done. First, "do not take revenge" for wrongdoing, but instead let God take care of matters. Then meet the physical needs of those around you. That's a pretty good way to start defusing trouble.

• "Make every effort to live in peace with all men and to be holy; without holiness no one will see the Lord. See to it that no one misses the grace of God and that no bitter root grows up to cause trouble and defile many" (Hebrews 12:14–15). When we pursue peace, follow God's moral commands, and weed out bitter emotions like pride, rivalry, and hatred, we can live at peace with just about anybody.

Yes, divisions may come, but you have new resources to assist you as you learn to use the peace you have with God to help create peace on earth among people.

A name that gives us access to God the Father. Prayer is something that many people talk about but not everyone can successfully use. We often hear about people who fire up a prayer toward God when a crisis hits. But the Bible tells us that not every prayer sent heavenward is answered.

Consider this verse. "No one comes to the Father except through me" (John 14:6). Jesus was talking to His disciples (His close followers) about heaven when one of the men asked Him how a person could know "the way." Jesus responded by saying that He is the Way and the Truth and the Life and that no one could have contact with God unless they went through Him. Access to God the Father is available only to those who have put their faith in Jesus Christ.

Jesus went on to say, "If you remain in me and my words remain in you, ask whatever you wish, and it will be given you" (John 15:7). Not only is it essential to be a follower of Jesus, but it is also important to remain in strong fellowship with Him if we want to communicate with God.

The avenue to God's presence through prayer, like the avenue to heaven itself, is not a wide boulevard open to all. It is a narrow channel through which only those can go who love and honor and trust God.

A word that means people will expect more from us. The story is told about a tennis player who toiled one afternoon for his Christian high school. In the heat of the battle, something upset him, and before he could stop himself, he blurted out some words that he immediately regretted. To his chagrin, those words were heard by fans from the other school. Immediately they began chanting, "What did you say, Christian? What did you say, Christian?"

People expect those who bear the name Christian to be different—to be better. Just as those high school students knew that it was uncharacteristic of a Christian for that tennis ace to loose his cool and say things he shouldn't have, so will some people expect certain behavior from you because of your new faith. It is at the same time a great honor and a humbling responsibility.

A name that means we are forgiven, but not perfect.
Like those tennis fans, there will be people who are
ready to ambush you. They will be hiding behind every lamp and listening through every wall, trying to
catch you being bad. Then they can haul out the
"Ah-ha's" and remind you that you aren't so great after all. "What kind of Christian are you?" they might
ask if they see you doing something wrong.

"A normal one," you can tell them.

Perfection is something believers can look forward to in heaven, but will never achieve on this
earth. Sure, we should do all we can to live for God
and avoid the troubles that sin brings our way, but
we won't be perfect.

This is how the apostle Paul described this
struggle: "For what I want to do I do not do, but what
I hate I do. . . . It is no longer I myself who do it, but
it is sin living in me. I know that nothing good lives
in me, that is, in my sinful nature. For I have the desire to do what is good, but I cannot carry it out. For
what I do is not the good I want to do; no, the evil I
do not want to do—this I keep on doing" (Romans
7:15, 17–19).

What is different about us is not that we are
perfect because we are saved, but that we have a
Holy Spirit-led desire within us to do what is right.
And then best of all, when we fail to accomplish our
goal of goodness, we are not left to suffer alone with
our sins clinging to us like parasites. First, we know
that our sins have been wiped from the record
through the blood of Jesus, so that they can never
be brought against us to deny us entrance into heav-
en. And second, we have a way to scrape off the parasites that hamper us in our lives here on this earth.

"If we confess our sins, he is faithful and just and will forgive us our sins and purify us from all unrighteousness" (1 John 1:9). Nobody who is perfect needs the opportunity to ask forgiveness. How important it is that we never think we have arrived spiritually—that we don't need the forgiveness that God offers.

A Christian nation?

A final observation about this new name may be helpful. For most of its history the United States has been considered a "Christian" nation. You may still hear people make that claim. This means that the country was founded on principles that can be best described as biblical, Christian principles. The Founding Fathers were not afraid to use the Bible to help frame their thinking, and that influence comes through in the basic principles of the government. This is not to say that all of the people who got this country started were Christians, but there was an underlying agreement that Christianity was right and that its teachings were the best basis for a new country.

Because of the respect people had for God, the Bible, and Christianity, schools taught the Ten Commandments, students said the Lord's Prayer, and God was viewed reverently. Literature generally respected the Bible, and biblical standards were, for the most part, upheld even into the early days of the electronic media.

But changes have come in our society. We live, some say, in a post-Christian era. As a new believer examining the media, the government, and education, you will discover that there is no longer a basic understanding of Christianity nor a feeling of good will toward it. You may find yourself put down, ridiculed, and treated as a second-class citizen. Not always will this happen, but you may encounter it more often than you'd like.

Remember that society has changed—the truth has not. Having stood the test of time for two thousand years, Christianity cannot be toppled by a mindset that has developed within the past thirty years or so. Just as Jesus declared that His church will stand and not even the gates of hell can defeat it (Matthew 16:18), so is the message of salvation never changing and always secure (Hebrews 5:9).

Wear the name Christian carefully, but wear it proudly.

Getting into the Word

What truths about the first-century believers in Jesus Christ can you gain from the following passages? What applications can you make to your life today after looking at these verses?
- John 4:39–42
- Acts 2:42–47
- Acts 4:32–33
- Galatians 6:10
- 1 Thessalonians 1:4–7
- 1 Timothy 2:1–6

Thinking it through

Consider the following questions as you reflect on what you have read in this chapter.
- What did you think of Christians before you accepted Jesus as your Savior? Were you right or wrong?

• Whom do you know who typifies what is wrong with Christians? What characteristics does this person have that turn non-Christians off?

• Whom do you know who typifies what is right with Christians? What characteristics do you see in other Christians that would you like to emulate?

• In what circumstances are you afraid to tell other people that you are a Christian? What frightens you the most, the possibility of ridicule? The fear of saying the wrong thing? A lack of background to defend your faith? What can you do to remedy this fear?

• How has your opinion changed of people who are not Christians, now that you are on the other side of the fence? Are you too harsh? Too tolerant?

Getting practical

Try these suggestions for applying what you have read.

• Write a letter to a friend and explain what has taken place in your life, emphasizing the fact that you are now a Christian.

• For several weeks, keep a diary of the reactions of people to you when you mention your faith.

• Look more carefully at how Christians are viewed in the media—newspaper, television, movies, music. Talk to someone who is older about how things have changed in the public perception of Christians.

Exploring the subject further

If you'd like to read more about what it means to bear the name *Christian*, these resources may help.

- *Mere Christianity*, C. S. Lewis
- *The Screwtape Letters*, C. S. Lewis
- *Knowing God*, J. I. Packer
- *How Should We Then Live?*, Francis Schaeffer
- *What We Believe*, John Walvoord

3

A Remarkable Relationship

*What can I do to keep my
relationship with God strong?*

When my wife and I brought our first child home,
our lives suddenly and drastically changed. Before
Lisa—and subsequently her two sisters and one
brother—our time outside of work was ours to do
whatever we wanted. On a Saturday, for instance, if
we wanted to sleep in all day, we could. Want to go
to the store? Just go. Our schedule was pretty much
open-ended.

The second we brought Lisa through those
apartment doors, a completely new way of operating
took effect. Our routine was regulated by new considerations, for we had the total responsibility of taking care of Lisa.

One might expect that we would have been irri-
tated that this little human had come in and turned
everything so topsy-turvey. How dare she demand so
much of us! How inconvenient that we had these extra responsibilities! How frustrating to have to share
our lives!

Is that how we felt? Absolutely not! It was our pleasure to serve this little gift from God and give of ourselves for her well-being. The addition of this new person in our lives would do nothing but make us better people. It was our joy to share the hours of our lives and the work of our hands with her.

You will meet people who wonder aloud how you can stand to be as dedicated to God as you want to be. You had life to yourself before, people will say. Why would you want to get yourself all involved now with this "religious stuff"? As new parents do, you will have to rearrange your schedule to fit in your times with God as your relationship with Him matures. Well-meaning friends and relatives may wonder why that is so important.

And so might you. Having understood that you needed to be rescued from sin by Jesus, you accepted His free gift of salvation. You may assume that you did all that was asked of you. Life can, you might think, go on as usual. Salvation is, you were told, a one-time event. Perhaps you figure that when you have taken care of it, there is little more to do.

Frankly, many Christians live that way. They are satisfied with a relationship with God that is best described as nominal. They are content to remain baby Christians, believers who never grow in their fellowship with God.

God's Word, though, suggests a far better way. The apostle Paul talked about taking the life of faith to new heights. Instead of living like the rest of the world, he told believers to "be made new in the attitude of your minds" (Ephesians 4:23). Paul issued a call for lives dedicated to knowing God better and living for Him completely.

If you are going to grow continually toward maturity as a believer, you will have to work at it. You will need to set aside time every day to read the Bible and to talk with God through prayer. These exercises will require discipline. But the work will not be drudgery. Rather, you will find that you know God better, that you serve Him more, that you experience His joy to a greater degree, and that your life is more in tune with His. Each day as you read God's Word and talk with Him you'll discover the heartwarming happiness and contentment of fellowship with the Creator.

Let's examine some ways these two disciplines can make a huge difference in your life.

Reading the Bible

As we will show in the next chapter, the Bible is like no other book. It does not have to be read front to back, straight through, as you would read something by Agatha Christie. That's an advantage as you get started because you don't have to get bogged down in one of the early books and never make it to the maps in the back!

Although the Bible contains some fascinating narrative that you may want to read in large chunks, it can also be read profitably in bits and snatches. For instance, if you want to read for specific help in your life as a new believer in Jesus, you could begin with a short book like Philippians. Or, if you like epigramatic sayings in short, easy-to-digest form, you could open up to a chapter in the Proverbs and get more help than you could probably use in one day.

This is not to say, however, that reading the Bible from Genesis, the first book, to Revelation, the last, cannot be done. Many new believers have been so excited to discover the details of God's plan that they have taken that path in reading the Bible. If you have the time and the inclination, that kind of effort would give you the best possible overview of God's Book.

Whichever way you choose to start reading the Bible, you may benefit by these suggestions for enhancing your initial times with God's Word.

Kinds of Bibles

Carefully consider the kind of Bible you want. You can get good translations of the Scripture in many forms. The King James Version was translated in 1611 and so uses a form of English that differs from the language of today, but many prefer it for its majestic sound. The *New International Version* is perhaps the best-known modern translation and may be the easiest to read. The *New King James Version* (a modern equivalent of the 1611 edition) and the *New American Standard Bible* are also widely used.

In addition to choosing a translation, you'll want to look at the typeface to see how readable it is to you; you'll want to check the Bible for its notes or lack of them; and you'll want to see whether or not it has a good concordance in the back. A concordance tells you where to find references to certain words. Notes will give you invaluable assistance if you want to study the Bible on your own beyond what you find in devotional guides.

A reading plan

Set aside a regular time for reading. Some people have even gone so far as to schedule a time each day for Bible reading by putting it in their Daytimers. This allows them to approach this special few minutes with God just as they would a regular appointment—cutting down on possible interruptions.

Settle on a plan. You might benefit from a daily devotional guide such as *My Utmost for His Highest* by Oswald Chambers, or *Our Daily Bread*. Such a tool helps you avoid the problem of knowing where to begin your reading each day. When I was managing editor of *Campus Journal,* a good devotional tool for young people, I received many letters from teenagers who said they always wanted to read the Bible but did not know where to start. With a devotional guide, you always have a reference point with which to begin each day.

You may want to also think of the value of reading through the entire Bible in a year. You can get schedules that divide the Bible into small segments that enable you to finish in 365 days. These schedules are often available in tract form and can be found at a Christian bookstore. Or you can simply start at the beginning of the Bible and read three chapters a day to cover the entire Scriptures in about a year.

Journaling

Keep a journal. Many of the great men and women of the church kept journals, not just of their Bible reading, but of their spiritual lives. David Brainerd, a great missionary of the eighteenth century, kept a fascinating journal. In it he chronicled his work among the Indians of North America and the observations he gleaned from his study of Scripture. One notable entry in his journal told of his diligence in setting aside time each day for fellowship with God. He called those daily efforts his "secret duties," a name that well describes both the privacy and the obligation of our Bible reading.

Your journal keeping will force you to do several things each day. First, it will require you to be accountable mentally for what you read. If you establish a pattern of writing down your thoughts and feelings upon reading the Bible, you will be less inclined to read the Word mindlessly.

Second, journaling gives you some reference points for later use. In effect, you will be writing your own mini-commentary on the Scriptures—one you can go back to at a different time for help in understanding a passage.

Third, your journal will allow you to plot the progress of your spiritual journey. In your journal, record how you are doing in obeying the truths presented in the Bible reading. Your goal is to make progress each day in being more Christlike and living by God's guidelines. Your journal will help you keep track of progress.

Fourth, your journal can be your own personal prayer list. List the things you want to pray about each day. Sometimes your list will include personal improvement requests that come out of the day's reading. Other times you may write praise notes stemming from a new discovery about God. You can keep your journal handy to jot down new items of praise and request during the day.

Talking to God
You turn on the news and you see that a famous person—perhaps a football player or a movie star—has

been injured. It will not surprise you to hear someone say, "Our prayers are with him." But if Barbara Walters is interviewing that celebrity about everyday life in which there is no crisis, the subject of prayer undoubtedly will not come up.

This imagined scenario points to the fact that for many people prayer is something to do when they get in trouble and have nowhere else to turn. They do not see prayer as a spiritual discipline that helps them get closer to God, but instead as an escape route to help them get out of trouble. It is good that these people find prayer helpful in extreme circumstances, but prayer is so much more.

Prayer may be new in your life now that you are a Christian, but it is every bit as important as reading the Bible. In fact, it complements Bible reading. Bible reading is God talking to you; prayer is you talking to God.

Before we get into the specifics of daily prayer times, let's take a good look at prayer and see who can pray, how to pray, why to pray, and what good prayer does.

Who can pray?

This may seem harsh, but Scripture indicates that there is a closed fraternity of people whose prayers are effective. The apostle Peter wrote, "The eyes of the Lord are on the righteous, and his ears are open to their prayer, but the face of the Lord is against those who do evil" (1 Peter 3:12). Of course, as a new believer in Jesus you can take comfort in knowing that you are in that group to whom God listens. But those who are not accounted righteous through faith in Jesus have no such assurance.

Also consider the following specific guidelines for how to pray. None of them pertain to the unrepentant; they apply only to those who trust Jesus Christ.

How should we pray?

Pray with a pure heart. "If I had cherished sin in my heart, the Lord would not have listened" (Psalm 66:18).

The Bible makes it clear that when people have sin in their hearts, God's ear is deaf to their prayers. In His message through the prophet Micah, God detailed the cruelties that rulers had committed against God's people. Because of what they had done God proclaimed, "They will cry out to the Lord, but he will not answer them; at that time he will hide his face from them because of the evil they have done" (Micah 3:4). It's not a popular message because we all want to have continual access to God, but the stipulation is clear.

If we want God to hear us, we must put 1 John 1:9 into action: we must confess our sins before we present our requests. Sometimes you might find yourself struggling with prayer, thinking it seems like trying to get through on a phone line that is constantly busy. At that point, do some self-evaluating and make sure it is not sin in your life that is cutting off the connection.

Go to God in faith. "When he asks, he must believe and not doubt, because he who doubts is like a wave of the sea, blown and tossed by the wind" (James 1:6).

A woman working as a missionary in India visited the town where a young orphan girl named Kara

lived. Kara was afraid that, because of her faith in
Jesus and her lowly social standing, she would be
forced into servitude. She pleaded with the missionary to take her back with her to live.

The woman sadly told Kara that she couldn't
take her. Her home was not big enough for another
person, and there wasn't any money to make it big-
ger. Before the missionary left, Kara told her that she
would be praying that God would make it possible
for the woman to take her in.

Upon returning to the mission station, the missionary found a letter from her hometown in the
United States, and it contained a large sum of money. Recognizing this gift as an answer to Kara's
prayer, she sent a messenger bring Kara to live with
her.

Within just a short time—much less time than
the trip to Kara's town and back should take—the
messenger arrived at the missionary's home with
Kara. Surprised, the woman asked how they could
be there so soon.

Kara answered, "When I prayed, God assured
me that it was His will for me to come to your home,
so I decided I might as well get started."

The messenger verified her story. "She was almost here when I met her."

Kara's testimony eloquently describes the
teaching of going to God in faith. Although we must
understand that not all of our requests will be answered so quickly, or exactly as we want them answered, we can't go wrong if we have a strong faith
that God always hears and responds.

In the New Testament we can read an example
of a group of people who did not have the faith in the

effectiveness of prayer that the young Indian woman did. This prayer story is recorded in Acts 12. It begins with a group of people praying for Peter, who had been thrown in jail by King Herod to cause trouble for the Christians (Acts 12:1). While Peter was in prison, his fellow believers got together at John Mark's mother's house to pray.

While they prayed, an angel appeared to Peter and freed him from the jail. Peter made his way to the house where everyone was praying, but when he arrived no one would believe it was Peter at the door! They were praying for Peter's release, but they seemed not to have the faith that their prayers could be answered.

One word of warning: some people misunderstand this instruction for praying in faith to mean that if you pray "right" you'll get whatever you want; if you don't get what you ask for, you must have been deficient in faith. Don't confuse prayer with a cosmic gumball machine—put in a quarter's worth of faith and automatically get a treat. It is always God who determines the answers to prayer, not we ourselves by our technique. Without presuming on God by expecting our requests always to be granted, we can pray in faith, looking expectantly for the answer and being ready to act upon whatever answer God provides.

Pray according to God's will. "This is the confidence we have in approaching God: that if we ask anything according to his will, he hears us" (1 John 5:14).

If this concept of "God's will" is new to you, it may need some explaining. It is a little like the will one sets up to dispose of an estate after one's death.

Of course God is not dead, and He is not dividing up the proceeds, but there is a similarity. God's will details the desires of His heart. Just as one's last will and testament describes one's wishes concerning the matter of one's estate, so does God's will describe His wishes for us.

You may hear people talk about God's will in matters such as trying to decide what job to take or whom to marry. But God's will also relates to some specific lifestyle guidelines that are spelled out in the Bible. For example, God's Word is clear that God hates lying; in the Ten Commandments and elsewhere we are told not to lie. It is God's will that we tell the truth. From this we know that a prayer which says, "Lord, help me to know what to say to Aunt Lillie. Should I tell her the truth about our reunion plans or should I make up a story?" is not a prayer prayed according to God's will.

That may sound a bit ridiculous, but it is all too accurate. It illustrates the importance of knowing what God's wishes are so that when we pray we honor them. By developing a clearer understanding of God's desires as expressed in the Bible, you can learn to pray as God wants you to.

Forgive others. "When you stand praying, if you hold anything against anyone, forgive him, so that your Father in heaven may forgive you your sins" (Mark 11:25).

One of the prayers that you may have known from memory even before you became a Christian is what we commonly call the Lord's Prayer. Jesus gave His listeners the Lord's Prayer when one of His disciples said, "Lord, teach us to pray" (Luke 11:1).

Leading by example rather than by lecture, Jesus simply said, "When you pray, say. . ." and led them in a short prayer. One of the elements of that model prayer is this line: "Forgive us our sins, for we also forgive everyone who sins against us" (Luke 11:4).

God, who has forgiven us so freely and completely, wants us to have that same attitude toward others before we begin to talk with Him.

Why pray?

In some ways, Christians are no different from anyone else. Believers in Jesus have to be convinced that there is a good reason for doing something before they are willing to commit their time and energy to it. When it comes to prayer, some of us never quite get convinced. We can easily decide that life will bump along just fine without working prayer into the mix. Sometimes we simply have not been shown enough substantial evidence to convince us that we need to pray.

We will not prosper from this unfortunate reasoning, for the Lord has supplied us with more than enough good reasons to pray—any one of which should be enough to convince us that we need to spend time talking to God.

We pray to obey God. When Jesus was on earth teaching His disciples, He often mentioned prayer. Luke, for example, records a story that was meant to teach the disciples "that they should always pray and not give up" (Luke 18:1).

The story is about a widow who continually asks a judge for justice in her situation. He at first refuses her request, but later, after the judge grows weary of her continual asking, he honors her request. Prayer, Jesus made clear, is not a fluffy, take-it-or-leave-it bauble. It is a vital means of communicating with God—and Jesus wants His followers to keep at it.

Unfortunately, the disciples sometimes had trouble doing that. We all do. Some of Jesus' disciples were with Him on the night He was captured by Roman soldiers shortly before His crucifixion. While they were in the Garden of Gethsemane, before the soldiers arrived, Jesus went away by Himself and prayed. When He returned, He discovered that His men were sleeping. Speaking directly to Peter, Jesus said, "Could you men not keep watch with me for one hour?" Then He told them why it was so important that they pray. "Watch and pray so that you will not fall into temptation. The spirit is willing, but the body is weak" (Matthew 26:40–41).

Jesus knew the situation, and He knew what His followers needed the most during this crisis night of their lives. He knew they needed to pray. We, too, have the command to pray, given to us through the apostle Paul. "Pray continually," he wrote (1 Thessalonians 5:17). It is a vital part of the plan God has for His children.

We pray to ask God for His help. The Bible is clear that God wants us to depend on Him for our well-being, and that one of the ways we depend on Him is through this avenue called prayer.

Look at the amazing ways prayer can help us:

• Giving us grace and mercy: "Let us then approach the throne of grace with confidence, so that we may receive mercy and find grace to help us in our time of need" (Hebrews 4:16).

• Relieving our anxiety: "Do not be anxious about anything, but in everything, by prayer and petition, with thanksgiving, present your requests to God" (Philippians 4:6).

• Introducing us to God's provision: "Ask and it will be given to you; seek and you will find; knock and the door will be opened to you. For everyone who asks receives; he who seeks finds; and to him who knocks, the door will be opened" (Luke 11:9–10).

We pray to praise and worship God. The simple fact that we have the opportunity to pray reminds us that God is a praiseworthy being. He alone in His greatness and love for us could give us such access. Although He created the universe with its astounding diversity and size and magnitude, He cares about each of us so much that He wants to communicate with us. When we contemplate just that combination of facts alone, we should find it easy to praise and worship Him. And prayer is one way we do that. An example of how we praise in prayer is found in the Lord's Prayer, mentioned earlier. The first thing Jesus told His disciples to say when they prayed was "Father, hallowed by Your name" (Luke 11:2). Our first statement of prayer should always be our recognition of His majesty.

Another good example of what we can say to praise God is found in Revelation 7. We glimpse the future as we listen in on how the inhabitants of heaven praise God. They say, "Praise and glory and wisdom and thanks and honor and power and strength be to our God for ever and ever" (Revelation

7:12). As you develop the habit of prayer, perhaps it will be helpful from time to time to recall this listing of God's characteristics and use them as your own prayer to Him. As you praise God with these words, the contemplation of them will allow you to worship Him in a fresh way.

We pray to keep the slate clean with God. Your first prayer of faith to God, the one in which you asked God to save you and to forgive you your sins, gave you something that can never be taken away. It gave you salvation through Jesus Christ. And that prayer also set you free from the penalty of sin, which is spiritual death and separation from God. It was a once-for-all prayer in regard to salvation. But one thing it did not give you was a lifetime of freedom from sin.

While we live here on this earth, we still sin, and we need continual forgiveness. We still miss the mark, we still do those things we know we shouldn't, and we still disappoint God. Here is where prayer comes to the rescue again. Because we want to keep our lines of communication open to Him, we will want to do as 1 John 1:9 tells us we should do: "If we confess our sins, he is faithful and just and will forgive us our sins and purify us from all unrighteousness." This is another kind of prayer—a prayer of repentance and sorrow. It is a request that we can never wear out, for we will need to go back over and over to God and ask His forgiveness. And it is a request we can never downplay, because our fellowship with God depends in part on our keeping a clean slate with God.

We pray to help others. One of the greatest charac-teristics of prayer is that it is a service opportunity. In chapter 9 we'll be looking at our responsibility to serve others, but we need to point out here that prayer is certainly near the top of any list of things we can do to help other people. You will meet elderly Christians who have discovered that prayer is their last great frontier of service. One ninety-year-old great-grandmother delighted that God had given her a bright mind despite her failing health, for she could spend many hours each day talking to Him about her family, her church, and the other needs of the Christian community.

The New Testament gives us some good exam-ples of how prayer for others is beneficial. The apos-tle Paul, when he wrote to the churches all over the Mediterranean seacoast, said things like this: "Since the day we heard about you, we have not stopped praying for you and asking God to fill you with the knowledge of his will through all spiritual wisdom and understanding" (Colossians 1:9). And he expect-ed prayer to be reciprocal, for he asked his fellow be-lievers at Thessalonica, "Finally, brothers, pray for us that the message of the Lord may spread rapidly and be honored" (2 Thessalonians 3:1). In the same way we can display our concern for our friends today by praying for their needs.

We have examined some of the details about prayer because it such an important foundational disci-pline for the Christian life. With a clearer under-standing of prayer, the task just begins, for this is not just a knowledge tool that we learn and store away. It is an action tool, one we need to keep out in the open and use regularly. Prayer may never come easily, and we may never seem to have enough time for it, but if we want real growth in our relationship with God we must make it a top priority today and for each day to come.

Getting into the Word

Look at these times Jesus prayed and note what you learn from His time alone with God.

- Luke 3:21–22
- Mark 1:35; Luke 4:42
- Luke 5:16
- Luke 6:12
- Matthew 14:23; Mark 6:46
- Luke 9:18
- Luke 9:28–29
- Matthew 11:25–27
- Luke 11:1–13
- John 11:41–42
- John 12:27–28
- John 17:1–26
- Matthew 26:39, 42, 44
- Luke 23:34
- Matthew 27:46
- Luke 23:46

Thinking it through

Consider the following questions as you reflect on what you have read in this chapter.

- Perhaps you've begun to read the Bible, but it sometimes does not make sense to you. What can you do, other than quitting, to lessen your frustration?
- Should you begin to set up a Bible reading schedule so that your reading is not hit and

miss? What is the best time of the day for you to read the Bible? What problems have you encountered already that you need to do something about?

• What are you looking for when you read the Bible? Would it help to ask these questions: What was God saying to the people of that day? What words or names should you look up? What truths from this passage can you take with you today as guidance? What do you remember from yesterday's reading?

• In your first attempts at prayer, what observations do you have about this exercise?

• If you have been having some trouble concentrating, should you do something about the time, location, or duration of your praying?

• Does it help you or hinder you to pray with other people?

• What kind of prayer do you pray most often? For others? For yourself? Praise to God? Confession?

• Have you begun the habit of starting a prayer list, perhaps with a column to check and record answers to prayer?

Getting practical

Try these suggestions for applying what you have read.

• Keep an appointment book in which you schedule time every day with God.

• If possible, set aside a special place in your home where the only thing you do is meet with God through prayer and Bible reading.

• Write a journal entry for each devotional session, writing down at least one challenge or lesson learned or blessing gained.

Exploring the subject further

The following resources can help you with the disciplines of Bible reading and prayer.

- *Enjoy Your Bible*, Irving L. Jensen
- *Our Daily Times with God*, Discovery House Publishers
- *Campus Journal* devotional from Radio Bible Class
- *Our Daily Bread* devotional from Radio Bible Class
- *Growing Strong in the Seasons of Life*, Charles R. Swindoll
- *My Utmost for His Highest*, Oswald Chambers
- *Prayer: A Holy Occupation*, Oswald Chambers

4

A Rock-Solid Foundation

What do I need to know?

The coach looks at his eager players assembled for the first day of football practice. They sit expectantly, waiting to hear the great wisdom their leader will unveil to them.

"Gentlemen," he says slowly, holding up a pigskin, "This is a football." Then, scanning the room carefully, he pauses and asks, "Any questions?"

This coach knows an important truth about teaching: start with the basics. He knows that he shouldn't assume that anyone knows anything, and that people learn complex concepts only if they first have a good foundation.

Every great football player who buckled his chinstrap and walked out onto the field at the Super Bowl was once a kid who had a coach explain to him what a forward pass is. A player will go no higher than PeeWee football without first building a foundation of knowledge about the game.

What is true of beginning football players is also true of beginning Christians. If you eventually want to be the kind of strong follower of Christ who can endure whatever ill winds might blow your way, you need to start by building a basic foundation of truth.

Without that foundation, you may find yourself falling victim to religious groups that will influence you to accept unbiblical teachings. As we see every time a dangerous cult crops up and destroys lives, that danger is very real. Cults and other religious groups often succeed in seducing Christians from the truth by presenting persuasive doctrines with enough elements of the truth to sound convincing—or at least confusing. For instance, a group might agree Jesus was a God—but not the one true God; or that personal faith in Jesus Christ is one way—but not the only way—to salvation.

To protect yourself you need to begin now to lay a foundation in truth. Then, any time you hear a statement that sounds strange, the Holy Spirit will be able to direct you to the true teachings that you know and away from the harmful ones that someone may be using to fool you.

One man who has set a good example for new believers is Chuck Colson. He accepted Jesus Christ as his Savior during perhaps the toughest days of his life, and he quickly began to build a solid foundation of Bible knowledge that has sustained him over the years. His faith was tested early in his days as a Christian because he was in the center of the Watergate controversy that brought down President Richard Nixon and sent Colson and several others to prison.

Colson began his search for God with the help of friends and through the reading of the book *Mere Christianity*; he continued his foundation-building through an intense self-instruction in God's Word. He began by writing down questions that he had always had about God, and he searched the Scriptures for answers. When he began his study, he knew only that Jesus was a historical figure; today Colson is one of the premier spokespersons for the faith. He has written many books that challenge and assist people of faith. It all began with a burning desire to know what the Book of books was saying.

Pete Maravich, who scored more points than anyone ever in college basketball, is another good example of someone who began with no knowledge of Scripture but dedicated himself to learning all he could from God's holy Word. After his ten-year career in the National Basketball Association was over, Pete began a search for the truth. His life was in disarray until he recalled the gospel story one night while agonizing over his own sadness. He prayed to God and asked to be saved. Digging into the Scriptures with the fervor he had once reserved for his efforts on the basketball court, he became a gifted speaker whose talks were punctuated with long passages of memorized Bible passages. When he died at age forty in 1988, he left behind a valuable legacy of faith.

Perhaps you are on the beginning side of such a quest. You are new in the faith or young in years and don't know how you can possibly achieve the biblical knowledge of a Colson or a Maravich.

Maybe when you sit listening to someone teach the Bible or preach, you feel frustrated. You know it won't do you any good to listen to someone expound on a complicated Bible doctrine like the Trinity if you don't know what the word *Trinity* means. On the other hand, you feel that it doesn't do any good to read a complicated book on doctrine, so you conclude, "I'll never understand this stuff!"

That feeling is understandable. But keep in mind that "this stuff" is simply the culmination of years of Bible knowledge. What you can do right now is to begin to lay a strong foundation of knowledge. On that foundation, as you read the Bible, study it, and seek the Spirit's guidance, you'll eventually construct a strong fortress of knowledge.

So where do you start? What is the equivalent for the new believer of "This is a football"? What truths are essential and fundamental to gaining a good understanding of God, His Word, and life on earth? The best place to start is with God, the Source of all knowledge, the Master of creation, and the Author of our salvation. Knowledge of God is basic to the maturing of faith.

Who is God?

Have you ever thought much about the first words of the Bible? The book of Genesis starts with, "In the beginning God created the heavens and the earth." This is a truly remarkable statement, full of things to contemplate. One notable characteristic is that this paragraph is about as good a newspaper lead as can be written. In ten words, it has four of the five elements that any crack newsperson wants in a story: *who, what, when, where.* The only one missing is *why,* but if God doesn't care to reveal His reason for creating the world, who are we to question Him?

Notice another thing in this classic opening sentence of the greatest Book ever written: it assumes that we know who God is. There is no attempt to introduce us to Him as if He were some character in a play that we need to have explained to us. There is no attempt to prove or argue His existence. In fact, the Bible nowhere tries to make a case for God's existence.

Despite the lack of introductory information about God, the Bible does not assume that we automatically know all we need to know about Him. Throughout the Scriptures we are given information about the God of the universe—information that helps us know Him as He wants us to, in a personal, direct way.

To begin developing the close relationship with God that is one of the goals of the Christian life, we can start by looking at His characteristics.

God is spirit

Have you ever heard people refer to God as some old guy in the sky with a long beard and a flowing white robe? That way of thinking about God is not only demeaning, it is impossible. The Bible tells us, "God is spirit, and his worshipers must worship in spirit and in truth" (John 4:24). We know God for His personality, His acts, and His love, but not for what He looks like.

God is eternal

This is where it gets really intriguing. God has existed forever. In our normal way of describing things, we say something that is really ancient is as old as the hills. In effect, we are saying that it is as old as the earth itself. That is indeed old. But now stop and think about Psalm 90:2. In that verse, the psalmist says of God, "Before the mountains were born or you brought forth the earth and the world, from everlasting to everlasting you are God." God is not as old as the hills, He is older than the hills. He is from everlasting.

Think about it. God had no beginning. His existence never had a start; He always was. Even before He created the heaven and earth God was there. Scientists who give the earth an age of millions and millions of years have nothing on God. The length of His existence makes millions of years look like nanoseconds.

The best part is that God not only didn't have a beginning, He will have no end. That's good news for everyone who has accepted Jesus as Savior, because God has promised eternal life to all who believe. God Himself will be present throughout that eternity. He will take care of us forever.

God is not a man

If we look back across history for a few good men and women, we can find them. There was Da Vinci, who was perhaps the greatest scientist, artist, and thinker of all time. There was Madame Curie, the brilliant chemist. There was Shakespeare, the writer who set the standard for all to follow. There were Thomas Jefferson, Ben Franklin, George Washington, and Abraham Lincoln—all brilliant statesmen. But all of these people, and every other one since Adam, were flawed. They were sinners. They were temporal. They were finite in their wisdom. They were, to put it best, just like us.

We worship One who is not like us. Listen to the words Moses used several thousand years ago to describe God: "God is not a man, that he should lie, nor a son of man, that he should change his mind. Does he speak and then not act? Does he promise and not fulfill?" (Numbers 23:19). God is Truth, and everything He says He will do, He does. God is perfect, and that sets Him apart from even the best human beings.

In the sometimes crazy world we live in, people often find strange objects and flawed beings to worship. We can have the confidence that our worship is not wasted on imperfection, that our faith is not in someone whimsical, that our love is given to One who truly understands it. Only one who is God can accept worship of one who is man.

God is personal

Do you remember your first prayer to God? Why did you bow your head and talk out loud? Whom did you expect to hear you? Whom did you expect to care about what you were saying?

Our prayers to God are indications that we believe this important characteristic about God: He is personal. We think He really does care that Uncle George is sick; that we need new tires for the car; that we want help with a relationship. We pray because we know that God hears our communication with Him and He somehow is going to answer us. God is not a man, but He is a person; He is personal.

God becomes grieved (Genesis 6:6); He can grow jealous (Deuteronomy 4:24); He becomes angry (1 Kings 11:9); He cares for you (1 Peter 5:7). All of these characteristics show us that God is personal. He desires a personal relationship with each of the people He has created.

God is loving

You might assume that you have always known this about God. Even before you came into the family of God and became personally acquainted with Him, you probably already knew the only portion of Scripture that many people know: "God is love" (1 John 4:16).

The problem with the almost universal knowledge of this characteristic is that it is also almost universally misunderstood. The statement God is love is a favorite of those who misinterpret *love* to mean "tolerance." People assume that if God loves so much He will tolerate all sorts of sinful behavior. After all, this thinking goes, anyone who is love must never punish, must never allow problems, must never judge, must never do anything but sit benignly by and watch people do whatever they want to do.

That is not what God's love is like. God's love was best demonstrated when He sent Jesus Christ to earth to die for our sins. "This is how God showed his love among us: He sent his one and only Son into the world that we might live through him" (1 John 4:9). God's love is a love that saw a people who were helplessly headed for a godless eternity. It is a love that led God to sacrifice His own dear Son for a race of people who are largely indifferent to this ultimate act of love. God in all His perfection and His care and compassion for humanity is the essence of love.

God is righteous

If God's love is the characteristic most widely accepted by even those who don't personally know Him, His righteousness may be the characteristic most people stumble over. If love implies tolerance, righteousness implies, to many, intolerance. How can God encompass both?

Look at it this way: Does a parent show love for his or her children by allowing them to do everything that pops into their mischievous little heads? Would an objective observer question a mother's love if she made her children do their homework when they didn't want to, or if she took a sharp object away from a child who was too young for it? Would an undisciplined lifestyle be approved by parents who truly loved their children?

Of course not. Likewise, God does not love a person any less when He asks for a commitment or when He punishes a wrongdoing. God is the King of the universe, and "righteousness and justice are the foundation of his throne" (Psalm 97:2). He rules the world with righteousness because He Himself is always right. And He rules with justice because He alone is just in all the world. A just ruling does not bring peace and happiness to someone who is guilty.

The God who is righteous is not a God who approves of evil. Evil occurs: Justice must be meted out. That is the way God maintains order in His universe.

Who is Jesus?

A second essential truth is the knowledge of who Jesus is. He, of course, is central to your faith, for it was in Jesus that you placed your faith when you became a Christian. But who is Jesus? And why does He alone have the power to save?

Jesus is a man

Jesus of Nazareth was a man. He was born of a woman in the same way every other person has been born since the children of Adam and Eve. He grew through the stages of childhood, youth, and adulthood in a normal fashion, as we can see by reading the records of His life (see Luke 2:52). While He was here on earth, He demonstrated the usual traits of humanity: He grew thirsty, He cried when He was sad, He grew tired, and He became angry.

Notice how the apostle Paul described Jesus. He said Jesus took "the very nature of a servant, being made in human likeness. And being found in appearance as a man, he humbled himself and became obedient to death—even death on a cross" (Philippians 2:7–8).

As with many today, some people in the first century had a hard time with the concept of God becoming human. They rationalized that Jesus didn't really take on human flesh and blood, He just took on the appearance of humanity. You can see how that argument might be convincing if the only passage we have about Jesus' humanity is Philippians 2. But the Bible gives us many other clear statements that Jesus was indeed truly and fully human.

Is that important? Let's see what God says, through the apostle John: "Every spirit that acknowledges that Jesus Christ has come in the flesh is from God, but every spirit that does not acknowledge Jesus is not from God. This is the spirit of the antichrist" (1 John 4:2–3).

Jesus is God

Yes, Jesus was a man who grew naturally through the stages of life, but He was at the same time God. He was the God-man, a unique entity who had existed forever as God and existed for thirty-three years on earth as a man. During those thirty-three years He set aside the glories of heaven, but He never set aside His deity. He was "in very nature God, but did not consider equality with God something to be grasped" (Philippians 2:6). That is why He could make Himself nothing (see Philippians 2:7) and take on humanity for those three-plus decades.

It is easy for most people to believe that the man Jesus lived, since historical records prove His existence. What is difficult for many is to believe that He is God. Here are a few lines of evidence that can help you accept this crucial truth about the Savior:

• *Jesus Himself claimed to be God.* Jesus said, "I and the Father are one" (John 10:30).

• *Paul made the claim for Him.* "For in Christ all the fullness of the Deity lives in bodily form" (Colossians 2:9).

• *Isaiah prophesied about Jesus the God-man.* "For to us a child is born, to us a son is given, and the government will be on his shoulders, and he will be called Wonderful Counselor, Mighty God, Everlasting Father" (Isaiah 9:6).

• *Jesus performed miracles in His own power that were recognized by His witnesses as coming from God.* "They were all filled with awe and praised God. 'A great prophet has appeared among us, ' they said. 'God has come to help his people' " (Luke 7:16).

Jesus is our loving Savior

Jesus was completely God and completely human at the same time. It is a mystery to us how that can be, but you will find that the greatness of God encompasses many things that we cannot understand. When we accept this truth and trust God's record that Jesus is God and human, we make some discoveries that will help us grow in our relationship with our Savior.

First, the fact that God would stoop to walk this dusty earth as one of us shows that He must truly love us. Second, the magnitude of His sacrifice on the cross becomes clearer when we understand that this gift of life eternal came at the cost of Jesus' pain and degradation before a mocking world—something He, as all-powerful God, could have easily stopped. Third, we can value even more our opportunity to have fellowship with the God of the universe—and that should make any Christian, whether a new believer or an old saint, do everything possible to enhance that personal relationship.

Who is the Holy Spirit?

The Holy Spirit is God

You may have noticed that we have covered only two of an important trio of names—God the Father and Jesus the Son—but we have said nothing about the Holy Spirit, who is the third person of the Trinity. The word *Trinity*, while not used in the Scriptures, reflects the biblical teaching that there is only one God, but He exists in three persons. Each of these three persons possesses all of the attributes of God, and all are equal in their divinity.

The Holy Spirit is our advocate

The Spirit is not some shadowy, passive member of the Trinity. He has been active since the beginning of the world. The Spirit was involved in Creation (Genesis 1:2). The Spirit inspired the writers of the Bible to pen the Holy Scriptures. The Spirit is still active today in many ways. He convicts sinners of their sin; He causes people who know Christ to develop bonds of relationship that those without Christ will never enjoy. "For we were all baptized by one Spirit into one body" explained Paul in 1 Corinthians 12:13.

Before He ascended into heaven, Jesus promised to send the Holy Spirit. He told His listeners that the heavenly Father would send them send a helper, and in Acts 2 you can read the story of how the Spirit came to the Christians. When the Holy Spirit came He did several things for those people— things He still does for Christians today:

- Gives us the power to witness (Acts 1:8).
- Helps us in our praying (Romans 8:26).
- Assists us in gaining knowledge (1 Corinthians 2:12).
- Helps us be the right kind of people (Galatians 5:22–23).
- Guides us away from sin (Galatians 5:16).
- Protects us because He is greater than the devil (1 John 4:4).

Christians have an advantage that no other people have. Perhaps people accuse you of using Christianity as a crutch. Don't let that bother you, for they don't know the half of it. The Holy Spirit's help is far greater than that of a crutch. As a believer, you have living within you one of the persons of the Deity, and He is always there to empower, protect, guide, and comfort you. When you need courage, He is there shore you up. When you are sad, He is there to encourage you. When you want to pray but can't, He is there talking to God on your behalf.

You could spend the rest of your life studying the triune God and you would never exhaust all that there is to know. On this foundation of knowing God rests everything else you need to understand about the Christian life. If you pursue God and seek to know Him better, you will be excited to discover His majesty and power, which will further amaze you when you consider that your heavenly Father is still concerned about you as an individual.

If you seek to know Jesus Christ as you read about Him in the Bible you will over and over be astounded at His wisdom and His love, and you will be challenged to emulate His care for those who were rejected by others.

If you seek to know the Holy Spirit by leaning on Him to help you make it through today and tomorrow, you will be energized by a power source that will never diminish. You will discover that, just as Jesus has the power to save you from your sin and deliver you from spiritual death through His salvation, so does the Holy Spirit have the power to lift you up and strengthen you to go forward into each day with confidence and hope.

As you seek to know God as He reveals Himself in these three persons of the Godhead, you will also discover new truths about the doctrines of the Christian faith, for it is God's Word that will guarantee you a foundation so solid it can never be shaken.

Getting into the Word
How do these verses suggest that there is more than one person in the Godhead?
- Genesis 1:26
- Genesis 3:22
- Genesis 11:7
- Isaiah 6:8

- Mark 1:9–11
- Matthew 28:19
- 2 Corinthians 13:14

How do these verses show that Jesus is God?

- John 1:1
- John 1:3
- John 8:58
- Philippians 2:6–8

What characteristics of God can we learn from these verses?

- Matthew 19:26
- Matthew 10:29–31
- John 4:24
- John 17:11

Thinking it through

Consider the following questions as you reflect on what you have read in this chapter.

- What is so important about gaining Bible knowledge? How will it help you to get the basics down?
- What confuses you the most when you try to put all of this together? Who can help you with your questions?
- What are you doing, besides going to church and reading the Bible, to build your Bible knowledge? Do you have any tapes of good Bible preachers? Do you have any books that can help? Are there any Christian radio broadcasts that might supplement your learning?

Getting practical

Try these suggestions for applying what you have read.

• Make a set of flashcards to help you learn the terms in Appendix A at the back of this book.

• Take a notebook to church to keep track of what the pastor is preaching about. You may find it helpful to write notes in your Bible so that when you come back to a passage you can benefit from an earlier teaching.

• Join a Bible study group that meets in a home. Many people benefit from getting together in small groups to learn.

• Some ministries offer Bible study curricula by mail. Perhaps someone at your church can direct you to such a group.

Exploring the subject further

The following books can help you build a strong foundation in the basics of Christian doctrine.

• *Growing Deep: Exploring the Roots of Our Faith*, Charles R. Swindoll

• *What We Believe*, John F. Walvoord

• *A Case for Christianity*, Colin Chapman

• *Eerdmans' Handbook to Christian Belief*, Robin Keeley (ed.)

• *Know What You Believe*, Paul E. Little

5

A Supernatural Book: Part One

How can I understand the Old Testament?

One of the things you may notice as you take your first steps as a new Christian is that suddenly everybody seems to be talking about the Bible.

When you go to church everyone seems to be carrying one around. During the service they all seem to know something about the Bible that you might not have discovered yet.

Like—where things are.

Strange things, like Habakkuk. And Philemon. The preacher mentions something unpronounceable and everybody dives into their Bibles, riffling through those thin pages to find the passage. When the preacher starts to read you may still be running your finger down the table of contents looking for Zephaniah.

The Bible is such an imposing work. You've read long books before, but this is the champion. More than fifteen hundred pages—without pictures. How will you ever get a handle on such a monumental piece of literature?

Is there some method to this manuscript mag-
nificence? Is there some way to get a grip on this
Book so it doesn't seem so overwhelming? What
should you know about the Bible, and how can you
get started reading it without being swept away by
its size?

Divide and conquer

Think about pizza for a moment. A pizza is a rather
large hunk of food. That's why Domino's and Pizza
Hut use those nifty pizza choppers to slice up your
saucy treat into manageable slices.

Can you imagine someone turning up his nose
at a Big Foot pizza because it's too big to eat? No, we
cut the thing up and eat it slice by slice. And if
there's too much, we put the rest in the fridge and
eat it tomorrow.

Yet there are people who refuse to read the Bible
because they feel it is too long.

There's no question about that—it is long!

It contains the history of humanity's existence
on earth (from the beginning until about two thousand years ago). It tells us everything God wants us
to know about the Israelites, His chosen people. It
gives us the condensed histories of people like Noah,
Abraham, King David, Jonah, Paul, and John the
Baptist. And it tells us all the things God chose for
us to know about the early life of Jesus Christ our
Savior. Yes, it is long.

But you don't have to read it all by tomorrow.

It'll keep.

Like a sixteen-inch pepperoni-and-sausage
marvel, the Bible has been portioned off to aid us in
our digestion of its contents. You can take your time

with it, one section at a time. The goal is to divide and conquer.

The ingredients

It's not usually safe to eat a pizza without knowing who made it and what it has inside. Likewise, it wouldn't be fair to ask you to accept the Bible without giving you some background about its contents. Truth in labeling being a major issue today, we don't want to take any chances. Here's what the label on the side of a Bible would say:

* Inspired by God (2 Timothy 3:16). Through humans who were touched by God in a special way to write down what He wanted them to say, God wrote the Bible.
* Contains sixty-six books, written by a widely diverse group of people, yet with one central theme: the human need for redemption and God's plan for it. It took forty authors approximately fifteen hundred years to write the Bible.
* Survived all attempts to destroy it. The Russians spent seventy-four years of this century trying to discredit it, finally to give up and begin printing it.
* Contains God's only plan for salvation.
* Tells us what God has in store for the future of the earth.
* Gives us some very clear guidelines for how to live.

Now that's a list that makes the government's daily nutritional requirements on the side of a box of Cheerios look rather bland.

The portions

Let's begin our enjoyment of God's Word by cutting it up into two major portions—the Old Testament and the New Testament. Then we can take each of those halves and slice them up into more manageable sections.

No one knows for sure how much historical ground the Old Testament covers as far as actual number of years are concerned, but one thing is for sure: *old* is a good word to describe it. The first three words of Genesis 1, the first chapter of the Bible, make that clear. They say, "In the beginning."

The Old Testament covers human history from the moment of Creation—and it gives evidence of God's existence even before that (see Psalm 90:1-2)—until four hundred years before Jesus arrived on earth in human form.

During that period of time several key events stand out. Those events, when understood in their context and sequence, will give you a good start in understanding the Old Testament.

Main events in Old Testament history

Perhaps the best way to gain a preliminary understanding of the Old Testament is to outline the key events of each book.

1. Creation of the universe—Genesis 1-2
2. Fall of man—Genesis 3
3. Noah and the Flood—Genesis 6-9
4. Founding of Israel—Genesis 12-23
5. Enslavement of Israel—Exodus 1
6. Deliverance through Moses—Exodus 2-12
7. Wilderness wanderings—Exodus, Numbers, Deuteronomy

8. Time of victory—Joshua
9. Rule of judges & kings—Judges, Ruth, 1 & 2 Samuel, 1 & 2 Kings, 1 & 2 Chronicles, Psalms, Proverbs, Song of Songs, Ecclesiastes
10. Exile & return of Israel—Ezra, Nehemiah, Esther
11. Time of the prophets—Isaiah through Malachi

As you begin to read small sections of the Old Testament (maybe over a pizza to remind you about the reason for manageable slices), you will notice a story unfolding—the story of what God wants you to know about humanity in general and the people of Israel in particular. Like Cliff's Notes for the Bible, here are some brief summaries that should help you understand what you are reading:

Creation of the universe: Genesis 1–2

Noted astronomer Carl Sagan has pondered life's biggest mystery and has concluded: "The cosmos is all there is." In other words, the distinguished star-gazer is saying that our earth and its neighboring galaxies came into existence without assistance.

He's not alone in his thinking. Many intelligent people hold to the theory that the existence of our planet and its riders is a matter of chance—that somehow it created itself. There is no room in this theory for God.

The Bible, however, starts from a far different perspective. It starts with God's powerful hand sweeping across the vast expanse of nothingness and calling the world into existence. Interesting, isn't it, that humanity's greatest question, "Where did we come from?" is God's first answer in Genesis.

Genesis 1 and 2 spell out, in simple terms, how things were "in the beginning."

Fall of man: Genesis 3

If you recall the discussion of salvation in chapter 1, you remember that the actions of two people thousands of years ago are still causing trouble today.

As our spiritual and physical progenitors, Adam and Eve set the spiritual tone for all of humankind when they failed to obey God's clear command. He told them not to eat the fruit of a certain tree, but they let Satan talk them into it. When they sinned, sin became a part of our heritage.

In explaining the results of their actions, God said, "The man has now become like one of us, knowing good and evil. He must not be allowed to reach out his hand and take also from the tree of life and eat, and live forever" (Genesis 3:22). Genesis 3 tells us how human beings came to be cut off from something we could have had—eternal life. Later in the Bible we will read how that problem can be solved for people one at a time.

Noah and the Flood: Genesis 6–9

The actions of the people who lived after Adam and Eve proved without a doubt that they had inherited a nature determined to do evil.

People, as a result of that sinful nature, could not help but sin. Imagine the sorrow this caused God—who created such majesty and beauty in the world and gave humans the opportunity to enjoy it in perfection.

The writer of Genesis described God's reaction vividly: "The LORD saw how great man's wickedness on the earth had become, and that every inclination of the thoughts of his heart was only evil all the time. The LORD was grieved that He had made man on the earth, and his heart was filled with pain" (6:5–6).

So grieved was God that He decided to start over.

Only one person seemed to be living the kind of life God designed—a man named Noah. He was a "righteous man, blameless among the people, and he walked with God" (6:9).

And because he was righteous, he not only walked with God, he sailed with Him, too.

God directed Noah to save his family and earth's animals by constructing a huge boat—big enough to accommodate two of each animal and still leave room for Noah, his wife, and his three sons and their wives.

Once these people and beasts were safely inside, God shut the door and sent a deluge of water to destroy the wicked people. This story—one of the best known of Bible events—symbolizes for us the salvation that we have in Christ that we read about in more detail in the New Testament. Only through faithful obedience to God could Noah and his family escape the watery judgment and live to repopulate the earth.

Founding of Israel: Genesis 12–23

Have you ever wondered why the tiny nation of Israel, which clings to life on the edge of the Mediterranean Sea, continues to survive? While her neighbors always seem ready to overwhelm her and push her people out into the sea, Israel maintains an uneasy peace—standing her ground against all who take her on.

By all rights the Jews should have ceased to exist long ago. They have been oppressed, uprooted, taken captive, persecuted, and maligned like no other group. For thousands of years, they have been victims of intolerance, violence, and hate.

So why have they not been annihilated like other groups in history? Mainly because they are, in God's eyes, a special people. He anointed them when He made a covenant with Abraham, the original Jew and the father of the Jewish people. And God has preserved the Jews through the centuries and has given them a key role in world events.

Part of the beauty of the Old Testament is the element of suspense that it carries with it. In several places the writers foretell the coming of a person who will save God's people. This great person, we learn, will be a descendant of Abraham—a Jew. One reason for God's preservation of Israel, at least through the first century AD, was because that nation was to produce the One who would save people of all nations.

But God's promises to Israel did not stop with the birth of Messiah Jesus. If so, those who have tried to destroy the Jews throughout history might have succeeded.

No, Israel was also promised a role of importance in a future society—one that will exist at God's command at the end of this present age.

As you read through the account of Israel's beginnings in Genesis, look for God's promises to the people. They will help you see why Israel is still so important today.

Enslavement of Israel: Exodus 1

It didn't take long for trouble to start for the people of Israel. The descendants of Abraham, the father of

Israel, left Canaan, the homeland God gave them, to escape a drought. Their search for food took them to Egypt, where an Israelite named Joseph had come to power as prime minister. The people of Israel settled in this new land and, for the next two hundred years or so, prospered.

But then a new king took the throne of Egypt. This pharaoh, as he was called, thought the Israelites were growing too numerous. He ordered them into slavery, putting cruel masters over them to force them to work.

Pharaoh's plan, though, had a flaw. He did not realize that he was dealing with a group of people who were especially favored in God's eyes. He did not know that God heard their cry for help (Exodus 2:24). He did not know about the man who, ironically, had grown up in the pharaoh's house and would be the only person who could stand up and force him to let the Israelites go.

Deliverance through Moses: Exodus 2–12

Moses had to deal with one tough pharaoh. In his drive to convince the Egyptian leader to let the Israelites get out of Egypt, Moses had to pull out all the stops. Here's a look at the things God did as Moses stood before the pharaoh to ask for freedom for His people:

- •Turned a staff into a snake
- •Turned the Nile River into blood
- •Plagued the land with a blanket of frogs
- •Sent gnats as numerous as the grains of sand
- •Unleashed swarms of flies over the land
- •Killed all of the livestock belonging to the Egyptians

•Afflicted the people and animals with boils
•Rained hail over the land of Egypt
•Sent locusts to devour the crops
•Darkened Egypt for three days
•Killed the firstborn of both people and animals in all Egypt, but protected the Jews.

With God guiding him, Moses overcame the pharaoh's recalcitrance and won freedom for his people. When the final plague hit the pharaoh's household—the plague of death that struck down the firstborn in his family—he at last relented. "Up! Leave my people, you and the Israelites!" the pharaoh told Moses and Moses' brother, Aaron, in a middle-of-the-night summons.

Moses quickly rounded up the people, collected clothing, gold, and silver from the Egyptians, and headed southeast toward the Red Sea. It was exactly 430 years to the day since the Israelites had entered Egypt. Six hundred thousand men, along with the women and children, were about to embark on an incredible journey.

Wilderness wanderings: Exodus, Numbers, Deuteronomy

Imagine the thrill the Israelites experienced as they left the land where they were slaves for so long. They were free, and they also had God's promise that they would be traveling to the land of Canaan, the land already promised to them (Genesis 15:13–16). Soon, they expected, they would enter their homeland.

Along the journey God had some important lessons He wanted to teach them—lessons in faith.

The people hadn't been out of Egypt very long before they began to have second thoughts about this trip. Despite the grand and impressive miracle that God did to allow them to cross the Red Sea just before a marauding band of Pharaoh's horsemen could get to them, the people began to lose their trust. First they ran out of water. Then they ran out of food.

God, however, never runs out of anything. So He changed bitter water into good drinking water. He sent quail for their food, and He followed that with a daily harvest of manna—bread straight from heaven. Often the people showed a tendency to forget that God was there to guide them and care for them. Yet despite their grumblings, God always took care of them. It was during this first part of the wilderness travels that a special day—a Sabbath day—was set aside for the people to worship God.

For almost an entire year the people camped at the base of Mount Sinai. While they were there, three significant events took place: they received the Ten Commandments (Exodus 19–24); they drifted from God into idolatry (Exodus 32); and they constructed the tabernacle (Exodus 25–31; 35–40; Leviticus 1–9; 16; 23), a visible place they could visit to worship God.

When the Sinai stay was over, the Israelites packed up and headed for Kadesh-barnea, where twelve spies were sent ahead to inspect the land that had been promised to them. Two of the inspectors came back and enthusiastically recommended that the land was ready to be taken. But ten of the spies did not think it was possible. Although the land seemed to have all the natural resources the people needed, the ten who doubted were afraid of being defeated in battle by enemy soldiers. The naysayers won out, and the people decided not to go into the land.

Because of this lack of faith, God vowed that none of the people who started out from Egypt would enter the land. As a result, the people spent the next forty years roaming the desert, unable to claim their Promised Land. At the end of those years, shortly after Moses died at the age of 120, the people and Joshua, their new leader, entered Canaan.

Time of victory: Joshua

For forty years, the people had been promised a land of their own to inhabit. Sometimes faithfully and sometimes reluctantly, the people followed the leadership of Moses, who brought them to the edge of the Promised Land. But it was Joshua who led them to their goal.

Imagine being in Joshua's sandals. Suddenly he was the leader of millions of people. Surely he must have wondered if he was up to the task. Yet God immediately gave him the confidence he needed by saying, "Be strong and courageous. Do not be terrified; do not be discouraged, for the Lord your God will be with you wherever you go" (Joshua 1:9). It is one thing for someone to encourage you to succeed; it is quite another for the encourager to also be the enabler. Joshua could do nothing but win with the help God was offering.

And win Israel did. After some exciting adventures in scouting out and claiming the land (read about it in Joshua 1–5), the Israelites went on the attack. In a series of campaigns, they conquered the land in various interesting ways, including the capture of Jericho through the strange strategy of walking around the city; the defeat of an alliance with the help of God-directed changes in the weather and the movement of the sun; and victory through disabling the enemy's horses.

After these victories, the Israelites settled in their new homeland, dividing it among the twelve tribes of people who made up the Israelite population. It seemed that they, assisted by God in their efforts to conquer the land, would finally have a long life of success that would give honor to the God of their deliverance. As the book ends, Joshua reminds them of all that God had done for them.

Rule of judges & kings: Judges, Ruth, 1 & 2 Samuel, 1 & 2 Kings, 1 & 2 Chronicles, Psalms, Proverbs, Ecclesiastes, Song of Songs

When the people of Israel settled in the Promised Land, they conquered all but one of the enemies that could have forced them out. And that one enemy territory remained unconquered because of the Israelites own stubbornness. The Lord told the people to destroy this remaining group, the Canaanites, totally (Deuteronomy 7:2). But the Israelites failed to take care of them. As a result, these wicked, pagan, corrupt people caused all kinds of trouble for God's people.

Still the Israelites were not content to do as they were told, nor were they willing to stop doing what they knew was wrong. They wanted independence from God. As Judges 17:6 explains, "In those days Israel had no king; everyone did as he saw fit." And what they saw fit to do was not what God wanted them to do. They turned their backs on the faith of their fathers, and they gave their allegiance to false gods such as Baal and Ashtoreth.

Over and over the people suffered defeat at the hands of nations such as Mesopotamia, Philistia, and Midian. Periodically a new judge arose to rule over the land, and Israel would enjoy a temporary time of peace and obedience to God. These good times, however, were inevitably followed by periods of disobedience and oppression. This hills-and-valleys existence lasted for approximately three hundred years. All the while, God demonstrated His mercy and patience by keeping Israel in the center of His love.

The people cried out to Samuel, a prophet of God who was the greatest of the judges of Israel, asking for a king. They were wrong in this request, for it indicated that they trusted a human being to give them the protection God Himself had promised them earlier. They wanted a king instead of being directly ruled by God.

Yet God did honor Israel's request. For the next 120 years after the time of the judges, Israel was ruled by three kings, each of whom served for 40 years: Saul, David, and Solomon. The stories of the three kings, presented in 1 Samuel (Saul), 2 Samuel, 1 Chronicles, Psalms (David), and 1 Kings and 2 Chronicles, Song of Solomon, and Ecclesiastes (Solomon), record an exciting array of ways God works in the hearts of those in power. Often the kings did not do what was right in God's eyes, but again and again God was longsuffering and loving with these men and the people they ruled.

This time of kings moved through two stages. The first, with Saul, David, and Solomon as rulers of a kingdom that was united, gave way to a much longer period of time during which the kingdom was divided into two parts: the northern kingdom, called Israel, and the southern kingdom, called Judah. This divided kingdom era was initiated during the reign of Solomon's son Rehoboam, and it continued until the land was overrun and taken captive by the Babylonians 460 years after Saul was named the first king.

Exile and return of Israel: Ezra, Nehemiah, Esther

Both kingdoms eventually grew indifferent to God's call, which came through various prophets, to repent and return to honoring Him. The northern kingdom fell first, to Assyria; the people eventually became a part of that nation, never again to have a separate identity. The southern kingdom fell later, to Babylon. These captives, however, retained their separate identity and were eventually allowed to go back to Jerusalem, their home.

Time of the prophets: Isaiah through Malachi

God called out special spokespersons who were His mouthpieces to the people of Palestine and the lands around it. They were called prophets, and they had various tasks. Sometimes they let rulers know what God's will was. Sometimes they preached righteousness. Sometimes they rebuked sinners. Sometimes they told of coming judgment. Sometimes they foretold events. Sometimes they talked about salvation. God's prophets diligently reminded the people of their covenant with God.

The greatest task of all, though, was that these prophets proclaimed the coming of the Messiah. Although they had no idea when He was coming, the prophets set the stage for the new era—the era of Jesus' life and death on earth for us.

Getting into the Word
These key verses help provide an overview of the Old Testament.

- Genesis 1:1
- Exodus 3:8
- Leviticus 11:45
- Numbers 14:6–10
- Deuteronomy 5:29
- Joshua 11:23
- Judges 17:6
- Ruth 1:16–17
- 1 Samuel 8:19–22
- 2 Samuel 5:12
- 1 Kings 12:19
- 2 Kings 17:22–23
- 1 Chronicles 16:31
- 2 Chronicles 7:14
- Nehemiah 4:6
- Esther 4:14
- Job 1:21
- Psalm 150:6
- Proverbs 9:10
- Ecclesiastes 12:13
- Isaiah 1:18
- Daniel 2:20–23

Thinking it through
Consider the following questions as you reflect on what you have read in this chapter.

- Why did God spend so much time in His Word talking about the Israelites? Why shouldn't

Christians focus only on the New Testament, where the story of Jesus and of salvation is told?
• What about the Old Testament sounds exciting to read?
• What will it take in the next year or so for you to gain a clear understanding of the Old Testament? What are you willing to invest in order for that to happen?

Getting practical

Try these suggestions for applying what you have read.

• Start a book-of-the-month club, with yourself as the only member. Set out to spend a month reading and studying each of these books of the Old Testament: Genesis, Exodus, Leviticus, Numbers, Deuteronomy, 1 Samuel, 2 Samuel, Proverbs, Isaiah, Jeremiah, and Daniel. Then move to other books in the Old Testament. Psalms will take longer than a month to digest, but others will take less time.
• Get an audiotape of the Old Testament to supplement your reading. It will help you stay with it when the narrative gets tough.

Exploring the subject further

The following books are good resources to help you with your understanding of the Old Testament.

• *A Popular Survey of the Old Testament*, Norman L. Geisler
• *The Heart of the Old Testament*, Ronald Youngblood

6

A Supernatural Book: Part Two

How can I understand the New Testament?

Perhaps it is nothing more profound than the name, but for many people the New Testament seems much more contemporary and approachable than the Old Testament. If both of these portions of the Bible strike you as being ancient, however, that is understandable. In our day and age, with everything moving and changing as fast as it does, a year as recent as 1945 seems like ancient history to many people. That's why it is almost unimaginable to think of something as being "new" that was written nearly two thousand years ago, before the Dark Ages, before there was an English language, and before Western civilization as we know it.

As you begin to read the New Testament, however, you will find it remarkably up-to-date. Sure, the stories are set in a different time and a different culture. You read about people walking and riding donkeys to their destinations. You picture them washing each other's feet because of the dusty roads. You read about a culture that is dependent on farming and fishing. Yet this God-inspired Book has been so timelessly crafted that you never feel that the message and the stories are exclusive to that time or culture. God in His infinite wisdom made sure the events and lessons of the New Testament were recorded in a way that transfers to any culture, any time period, any place.

One thing that marks the difference between the two testaments is the fact that the New Testament ushers us into a different era of the history of God's plan. Recording the story of Jesus' life and sacrificial death, this section of Scripture moves us from a system of law that we have a hard time understanding to a system of grace that is the same for us today as it was for the people to whom the New Testament letters were written. The Old Testament is the story of the Jews, but the New Testament is the story of all who have accepted Jesus Christ as Savior.

How do we know the message of the New Testament was written so directly for us? A couple of passages in the gospel of John can help us see that the future church of Jesus Christ (of which you are now a part because of your salvation) was on Jesus' mind. One of those passages is a prayer He prayed just before He was arrested and taken away by Roman soldiers to be put on trial. After praying for Himself and for His disciples, Jesus said, "My prayer is not for them alone. I pray also for those who will believe in me through their message" (John 17:20). Here is a clear reference to each of us who through the past two thousand years have put our faith and trust in Christ.

The second reference to us is in John 20:29. We can almost see Jesus looking past His disciple Thomas to smile at us as He said, "Because you have seen me, you have believed; blessed are those who have not seen and yet have believed."

That's us. We have not seen Jesus face-to-face, yet we put our heartfelt trust in Him to rescue us. Our faith in a person we know but cannot see makes us, Jesus promised, "blessed."

Finally, we can feel the encouraging reality of a message prepared just for us when we read the last verse of John 20. The writer of the book, almost as an apology for not recording more "miraculous signs" that Jesus provided His followers, said the things he wrote were done for us for a reason. "These are written," he penned, "that you may believe that Jesus is the Christ, the Son of God, and that by believing you may have life in his name" (20:31).

Indeed the message of the New Testament transcends the generations that have passed between the days of Jesus' life on earth and today. The New Testament contains up-to-date information on such concerns as how to be a good husband or wife, how to get along with people in the church, how to conduct ourselves in our daily conversation, the right attitude toward sex, how to respond to people in authority over us, and what to do about people who are less fortunate materially than we are. The New Testament is alive with help for us today. Amazing as it seems, this two-thousand-year-old book is as modern as any message on the latest computer bulletin board.

Besides that, the New Testament is good reading. Shorter by far than the Old Testament, it is more manageable and less imposing. And because it is so full of application to life today, you'll find yourself going back to favorite parts of it over and over.

But perhaps it is too soon for you to think in those terms. If the New Testament is brand new to you, maybe you first need the same kind of sketch that we gave of the Old Testament. Let's look at an outline of the New Testament.

The Gospels: the story of Jesus

Teeming with true stories about Jesus' life, as well as stories He told to illustrate His points, the four books that we call the Gospels—Matthew, Mark, Luke, and John—record everything God wants us to know about the Savior's thirty-three years of earthly ministry. As biographies go, some might say that these four accounts leave too much to the imagination. For instance, what we know about the details of Jesus' life can be summed up in very short order. We know:

• The facts surrounding His birth.

• That when He was a baby His parents had to flee the country with Him because King Herod was trying to kill Him.

• That as a twelve-year-old Jesus was accidentally left behind by His parents; He stood in the temple and amazed the religious teachers with His knowledge.

• That His earthly ministry began at the age of thirty.

• That He spent His last three years performing miracles, preaching His message, and preparing a group of people to spread the gospel when He was gone.

• That He lived sinlessly, yet was executed on a Roman implement of capital punishment, a cross.

• That He died, yet three days later rose again and appeared to hundreds of eyewitnesses over a period of days before He ascended into heaven, where He still is today.

As you read the Gospels, you will notice some repetition. Matthew, Mark, and Luke are called the "Synoptic Gospels." The word *synoptic* means to see the whole together. In other words, the first three books of the New Testament give us a comprehensive look at the life of Christ. Each author recorded many of the same events, yet told them from a bit of a different perspective.

For instance, the gospel of Mark has an energetic feel to it. Written in a succinct, fast-paced style, it moves along quicker—with fewer details than either Matthew or Luke give.

The fourth gospel, written by John, is quite different from the first three in structure, content, and style. It was written by a man who knew Jesus perhaps better than anyone else did. The author called himself "the disciple whom Jesus loved" (John 13:23).

Often today we read biographies written by people who were allowed to spend a couple of weeks or perhaps a full sports season with a famous person to write a story. John did better than that. He was Jesus' companion day in and day out. Unlike a modern biographer, whose close relationship with his or her subject provides lots of observations of the subject's faults, John contended strongly that his subject was sinless—and more than that, was God.

The Gospels are the foundational books to read as you become familiar with the New Testament. The Old Testament shows how God worked through His chosen people, the Israelites; the New Testament shows how God's plan of salvation gives hope to all people. The story laid out in the Gospels gives meaning to the other twenty-three books in New Testament.

Let's look in more detail at what the Gospels tell us about Jesus.

The birth of Jesus: Luke 2:1–7; Matthew 1:18–2:12

Unlike any baby ever born before, Jesus was unique. He was conceived by a woman who had never had sexual relations with a man, long before this modern era of in vitro fertilization and artificial insemination. His coming birth was announced by angels, and after He was born His arrival was heralded by celestial singing and wonders.

The baptism of Jesus: Matthew 3:13–17; Mark 1:9–11; Luke 3:21–22; John 1:31–34

A man called John the Baptist was traveling throughout the countryside telling people that the Messiah was coming. When Jesus went down with John into the water to be baptized, He let people know that John's message was true.

When Jesus came up out of the water after being baptized, two things happened. First, "heaven was opened, and he saw the Spirit of God descending like a dove" (Matthew 3:16). Second, "a voice from heaven said, 'This is my Son, whom I love; with him I am well pleased" (3:17). At the scene, then, were all three persons of the triune God—the Trinity.

The temptation of Jesus: Matthew 4:1–11; Mark 1:12–13; Luke 4:1–13

Because Jesus was fully human, we have the comfort of knowing that He, like all human beings, endured temptation. When we face situations that could lead us to sin, we know that Jesus understands what we are going through. In fact, the temptations that He faced were greater by far than anything we will ever encounter. And He passed the test. In so doing He proved His sinlessness, which qualified Him to be the only possible sacrifice for our sins, and He gave us a model to follow when sin tempts us.

The teachings of Jesus: Matthew 5–7; Luke 6:20–49

Jesus was called "Teacher" by many who knew Him, which is not surprising considering the profound and clear teachings He gave His listeners, starting with the Sermon on the Mount, continuing with the instruction called the Lord's Prayer, and moving through the many parables.

The first miracle of Jesus: John 2:1–11

When Jesus turned water into wine at a wedding feast, it was the first of many, many miracles that He performed during His three years of ministry. During the days to follow, the miracles were perhaps more astounding, yet this one is no less important. For one, it showed His care and concern for the small needs of people, as He saved the family the embarrassment of running out of wine for their guests. Jesus' presence at the wedding suggests that

He gives His endorsement to this God-given institution. But most significantly, this first miracle inaugurates the new era of the promised Messiah, for abundant wine is a symbol of God's restoration of His people (Amos 9:14).

Jesus and Nicodemus: John 3:1–21

If you are concerned about a friend who doesn't know Jesus as Savior, you might encourage that person her to read the gospel of John. But if you want to start with a shorter passage and you want the one that may be most convincing, suggest John 3. Here Jesus put it all on the line for a man who wanted to know about this salvation that Jesus was offering. This account contains the all-important command: "You must be born again" (3:7). And this chapter contains the all-important verse: John 3:16. We can see in the interaction of Jesus and Nicodemus the clear claims of the gospel.

The Lord's Supper: Matthew 26:20–29; Mark 14:17–25; Luke 22:14–20; John 13–14

Toward the end of Jesus' ministry on earth, He met with His disciples in a special room to enjoy a farewell meal with them. Although He had been trying to tell them that He would soon be crucified, they didn't get it. It was at this supper that Jesus identified Judas as His betrayer, predicted that Peter would deny Him, promised to prepare a heavenly home, explained the way to God, promised to send the Holy Spirit, and instituted the communion that believers still celebrate today. Jesus had many final remarks for His disciples, as well as a long prayer for them and those of us who would follow. It was a remarkable evening in that upper room.

The crucifixion of Jesus: Matthew 27:33–66; Mark 15:21–47; Luke 23:33–56; John 19:17–42

The events recorded in the final chapters of all four gospels are not the triumphant and glorious happenings that we would expect the King of kings and Lord of lords to face. Shouldn't He be lifted up and worshiped, glorified and praised, lionized and honored? Yes, He should. And He will be.

But the last parts of the Gospels are not the last chapters of the history that God is writing. These pages that are filled with the sorrowful story of Jesus' cruel and inhumane death contain, in fact, the central event in the total plan of God—an event that in its tragedy seems to suggest failure but instead leads to victory. Yes, Jesus could have skipped this week of horror in His earthly life. He could have gone back to heaven unscathed. But if He had, the final great and magnificent victory, which will include all of us who have been freed through His sacrifice, could never have been assured.

That's the good in Good Friday, the day of the Crucifixion. Because of Jesus' sacrifice and willingness to die, we have life.

The resurrection of Jesus: Matthew 28:1–7; Mark 16:1–8; Luke 24:1–10; John 20:1–18

Had Jesus stayed in the tomb, the gospel would have no power. A dead savior is no savior at all. To prove His power to save and redeem, Jesus has to be alive. He has to have the power over death. He has to be alive to fulfill His prophecies about Himself. The resurrection of Jesus, which is verified by many evidences in Scripture, reinvigorated Jesus' friends and sent them out into the world to proclaim the hope of the Christian faith.

Acts: the founding of the church

Jesus' physical work on earth was over. He had done what He came to earth to do, and you might think that the message of the New Testament would be over as well. After all, before we get ten verses into the book called The Acts of the Apostles, Jesus is gone.

As the disciples stood and watched, the Man they followed for three years was taken up into the heavens. It would make a dramatic ending to any story—a triumph of good over evil and an exciting conclusion to the greatest story ever told.

You could almost expect the book to conclude right here—for what else could there be to anticipate with Jesus gone?

But this is where it really begins to get exciting for us. Remember that Jesus promised His friends that when He left He would send a Helper to them. Now that He had ascended into heaven, it was time for that promise to come true.

This helper, whom we know as the Holy Spirit, came to indwell, or to live within, each believer. No longer did the people have to depend on being in close proximity to Jesus to feel His presence. Soon, the Spirit arrived to empower each believer individually—a function He still serves today.

Just as the people of those days had the promised help of the Holy Spirit, so do we. The events recorded in the rest of the book of Acts tell us what happened when the followers of Jesus were touched by the Spirit of God.

The power arrives: Acts 2:1–40

It was a Jewish day of celebration, the Day of Pentecost. The disciples gathered to honor this tradition;

suddenly something unusual and perhaps frightening occurred. The sound of a strong wind swept through the place where they had assembled, and something that looked like tiny fires appeared on their heads. Imagine their surprise when, in addition to these strange occurrences, they suddenly found that they could speak languages they had never learned.

The sound of the wind was apparently heard by Jewish people who were visiting from out of town, and they came to see what was going on. Astoundingly, the disciples communicated with those people in their own languages. The crowds were amazed. Some asked "What does this mean?" Others just thought the disciples were drunk.

But soon they heard the sober truth from Peter. Answering the question, "What does this mean?" Peter stood and delivered the first sermon of the Christian church. Apparently unrehearsed, yet guided by this new power that had come to the disciples, Peter preached a rousing message that ended with a call for repentance. Boldly, this man, who just seven weeks before had been afraid to tell a young girl that he knew Jesus, left no doubt about the importance of trusting Jesus as Savior.

The church is born: Acts 2:41–3:26

Three thousand people responded to Peter's message. Just like that, there was a three-thousand-member congregation to take care of, and the number continued to grow. Immediately the people developed a unity that must have startled the unbelievers. They had fellowship. They took communion. They saw miraculous things done. They shared their possessions. They praised God together. And they saw even more people accept Jesus as Savior.

The church is attacked: Acts 4:1–8:3

It would be nice if a world of peace and happiness had followed the founding of the Christian church, but that's not what happened. Whenever the work of God gets going, opposition springs up because there is a force in the world that does not like God and His plan. In the case of this new church in the first century, opposition began when Peter and John were arrested for preaching and were given some heavy reprimands by the religious leaders.

The worst personal attacks were reserved for a man named Stephen. Chosen as one of seven men who were to be leaders in the church, he is described in Acts as a person full of faith, full of the Holy Spirit, and full of God's grace (6:5, 8). Yet, like Peter and John, Stephen annoyed the religious leaders because of his faith.

So the religious leaders set up a scam in which some people claimed that they heard Stephen blaspheme God. These false witnesses also testified that Stephen was doing other things that went against Jewish custom and tradition. Against those accusations, Stephen gave a rousing speech in which he rehearsed the history of the Jewish nation. His recounting of historical facts didn't get him into trouble, but his final remarks did. He accused the council who was judging him, saying that they were responsible for killing Jesus and that they disobeyed the law. Infuriated, the council became a mob that took Stephen out and stoned him to death.

As the stones fell upon Stephen, he cried out to God, saying, "Do not hold this sin against them" (7:60). With forgiveness on his lips, he died, becoming the first martyr for the cause of Jesus Christ.

He was not alone in his trouble. Not content with what they had done to Stephen, his persecutors went after all of the new converts to Christianity. Men and women were taken from their homes and thrown into prison for their beliefs. Those not captured were "scattered throughout Judea and Samaria" (8:1). But the plan of the persecutors backfired, for those Christians who moved out into other areas "preached the word wherever they went" (8:4).

The church of Jesus Christ, of which we are now a part, began its worldwide spread—thanks to people who wanted to stop it.

The greatest missionary: Acts 9–28

One person who played a large part in both stoning Stephen and persecuting the church was a man named Saul. If one thing characterized Saul, it was his hatred for Christians.

Yet in what is perhaps the greatest personal turnaround of all time, this individual eventually became the most influential Christian in the first century. And his influence continues today in the many books of the Bible that God inspired him to write.

We know him now as Paul the apostle. After being stopped by a blinding light and the voice of the Lord, Saul turned his life over to Jesus Christ. With the same measure of passion that once drove him to stop the church from growing, he was invigorated to help it grow. For the rest of his life he traveled the region preaching the gospel and instructing the churches. He was beaten, thrown in jail, ridiculed, and shipwrecked during his ministry, yet he continued—setting an example we can all learn from as we face our own battles. The remainder of the book of Acts describes the journeys, the successes, and the difficulties Paul faced.

Letters: instruction to the church

As new Christians went throughout the Middle East and parts of what is now Europe—some seeking new homes, some spreading the message of the gospel as missionaries—groups of believers sprang up to form a network of churches. Because this faith was new to all of these groups, they had no uniform way of knowing exactly how the Christian life was to be lived. They had no New Testament to instruct them, no set of guidelines for living. Other than the individual promptings by the Holy Spirit, these new Christians had little direction.

The best way to give instruction to these churches was through letters. So Paul, James, Peter, John, and Jude wrote a total of twenty-one letters that were sent throughout the region—letters that gave both doctrinal teachings on what to believe and practical instructions for how to live.

Each letter emphasized a somewhat different theme that the writer knew the church needed to hear about. Today as we read the entire set of twenty-one letters, we can establish a clear set of guidelines for belief and practice. The instructions found in the letters are not out-of-date or obsolete. They have a timelessness and applicability to today that is astonishing.

Let's look briefly at what each letter to the churches emphasizes:

- Romans: God's plan of salvation, which brings righteousness
- 1 Corinthians: Errors of conduct in the church
- 2 Corinthians: Defense of Paul's authority and integrity
- Galatians: Justification through faith, not works
- Ephesians: What Christians have as believers
- Philippians: Christ's humility; the Christian's contentment
- Colossians: Refuting heresy by honoring Christ
- 1 Thessalonians: The return of Jesus Christ
- 2 Thessalonians: Encouragement and exhortation
- 1 Timothy: How to run a church
- 2 Timothy: Final words to a close friend
- Titus: Instructions about faith and conduct
- Philemon: The story of Onesimus
- Hebrews: Christ the supreme One
- James: Practical Christian living
- 1 Peter: Holiness, submission, Christian conduct
- 2 Peter: Christian growth in view of Christ's return
- 1 John: Assurance of salvation
- 2 John: Avoiding false teachers
- 3 John: Commendation of true teachers
- Jude: Warning about false teachers

Revelation: a look back; a look ahead

When we read a book of the Bible, we know that what it says is true because it was "God-breathed" or *inspired* by God. Somehow, in a process that we may never clearly understand, God prompted the people who penned His Book to write what He wanted them to write.

Revelation, the last book of the Bible, gives us a rare insight into how God communicated His message to the writer. The substance of this book was given to the author, John, in a collection of visions and dreams. Notice how the book begins: "The revelation of Jesus Christ, which God gave him to show his servants what must soon take place. He made it known by sending his angel to his servant John, who testifies to everything he saw" (1:1–2).

The message John received was a combination of a look back at some problems in seven early churches and a look forward to heaven and the end of this earth as we know it.

A look back: Revelation 1–3

In John's vision, Jesus Christ Himself delivered a message for seven churches that were located east of the Aegean Sea and north of the Mediterranean. Some of the churches were doing what they should and others were not. The first chapters of Revelation make up a kind of report card for these seven congregations.

A look ahead: Revelation 4–21

Heaven. It is the ultimate prize for the believer in Jesus Christ—a symbol of hope and eternal love. Imagine John's amazement as he saw the vision of heaven that is detailed in chapter 4. He saw the throne of God, heard heavenly creatures singing, and witnessed the worship of God.

The vision continues for John—and for us as we read it—taking us through a dizzying array of symbols and events that represent the future of the church.

While most of the New Testament books are straightforward narrative or exposition presented in a nonsymbolic way, Revelation is much more complex. Ordinary first-century objects such as seals and trumpets and scrolls take on new and sometimes difficult-to-understand symbolism. You'll find that you understand the book of Revelation better if you use commentaries or Bible encyclopedias that can explain what is not easy to figure out.

The final comforting message from Jesus, however, is clear and certain for every reader to understand. "Yes, I am coming soon," He proclaims. As you work your way through the book of Revelation, there will be times when you are not sure how to interpret what you read. But you can rest assured that the great message at the end is indisputable. Jesus is coming to earth again; and that's His final promise.

Getting into the Word
Each of the following passages presents an important event in the life of Jesus. Look up each passage and summarize the event described.
- Luke 2:1–7
- Luke 2:21–38
- Matthew 2:13–23
- Luke 2:41–50
- Matthew 3:13–17
- Matthew 4:1–11
- John 1:29

- John 2:13–25
- John 3:1–21
- Matthew 10:1–4
- Matthew 16:13–20
- Matthew 17:1–13
- Matthew 21:1–11
- Matthew 23:37–39
- John 13:1–14
- John 18:1–11
- John 18:12–19:15
- John 19:16–18
- Matthew 28:1–7
- Luke 24:51

Thinking it through

Consider the following questions as you reflect on what you have read in this chapter.

- In reading through this chapter on the New Testament, what has been the most surprising observation to you?
- What challenges in your life do you see being answered through the teachings of the New Testament? Where do you start in working through those challenges?
- What parts of the New Testament should you spend the most time in first—the Gospels, the letters, or Revelation?

Getting practical

Try these suggestions for applying what you have read.

- Choose one of the four Gospels as the one biography you will read this year. Set up a schedule for making sure you read it. As you read each chapter, write down a phrase that summarizes what that chapter is about.

• As you go through the New Testament, whether you are reading it alone, listening to it being preached, or participating in a Bible study, highlight or mark each verse that can be applied to your life. Mark these passages as "Lifestyle Christianity" verses to remind yourself that the New Testament is our guide for daily living.

• Memorize the names of the twenty-seven books in the New Testament and familiarize yourself with where each is. This will help you follow along when a preacher makes reference to the New Testament.

• As with the Old Testament, get a series of audiotapes to listen to as you read the New Testament.

Exploring the subject further

The following books can enhance your understanding of the New Testament.

• *Basic Introduction to the New Testament*, John R.W. Stott

• *How to Read the Gospels and Acts*, Joel B. Green

• *New Unger's Bible Handbook*, Gary Larson (ed.)

• *The Message*, Eugene Peterson

• *The Dramatized New Testament*, Michael Perry

7

A Different Way of Life

How do I live for God?

Have you ever met someone who is a genius, yet has no people skills? Perhaps it is a brilliant scientist who hasn't got a clue about how to conduct himself at a dinner party. Or a computer expert who can't get along with anybody who doesn't talk Applespeak.

We will be just as lacking spiritually as some people are socially if we fail to realize that simply gaining a basic understanding of the Bible is not enough. We have to go beyond knowing the Word— we must live it.

As a new believer in Jesus, you have the challenge of a lifetime ahead of you. It is the challenge to live a life that is different from the one you lived before you professed faith in Jesus. You are a new creation, and the old stuff has died off. Everything is new and fresh. That should affect the way you live. Even if you now understand basic doctrines and have a general understanding of Scripture, you haven't yet completed the task. The real job is living as God would have you live. Anything else is like being a great scientist but a lousy person.

So how does this happen?

Two essentials: power and training

If this new life of faith is indeed going to be different,
you need to incorporate two things in your daily
schedule: the help of the Holy Spirit, and some good
training from the Word of God.

Without these two components, you'll face frustration and failure in your attempts at Christian living. With them, you'll find joy and peace that are
unattainable in your own power.

For proof of that, let's look at a couple of passages in the New Testament. In Romans, for example,
Paul wrote these words: "May the God of hope fill you
with all joy and peace as you trust in him, so that
you may overflow with hope by the power of the Holy
Spirit" (Romans 15:13). In this life, only the Holy
Spirit can empower us in spiritual matters, and any
attempt to live as a Christian without His help won't
work.

Now look at a second passage, John 15:10-11.
Here, Jesus is giving some instructions to His followers. Notice what He says about the basis for their
training as they attempt to live for Him, and how
closely this relates to their potential to find true happiness. "If you obey my commands, you will remain
in my love, just as I have obeyed my Father's commands and remain in His love. I have told you this
so that my joy may be in you and that your joy may
be complete."

The Holy Spirit's help.

The training of God's commandments.

Two essential components to successful daily
Christian living.

Perhaps an illustration adapted from a scenario
suggested by author Richard Foster can help explain

why the basis of living for Jesus is found in the power of the Spirit and the training of the individual.

Suppose there is a marathon, twenty-six miles, planned for tomorrow morning and I want you to run in it. You are enthusiastic enough to give it a try, so you show up early on race day in your Nikes, your compression shorts, your runner's T-shirt—all set to go. I give you a pep talk and tell you that you can do it. Sure, you are a new runner, but why should that slow you down? I tell you how much I am depending on you to finish this race. Excitement surges inside you as you listen, for you believe you can do it and you are totally dedicated to giving it your best. You are ready to go for it.

We head for the starting line, and you tell me not to worry. You're going to give it your best. You want to run, and you are dedicated.

Convinced of your sincerity and your determination, you take your position. The starter fires the pistol and off you go. You make it up the first little hill and glide down out of sight of the starting line. Before too long you are within viewing distance of the first mile marker. But something is wrong. You are starting to slow down. Your lungs hurt. Your feet are killing you. Your legs feel like anvils. Before you make it to the first milepost, you collapse to the road, huffing and puffing. You are exhausted, embarrassed, and defeated.

What went wrong? Weren't you trying? Didn't you care?

Of course you did. But what was wrong was that you neither had the power—no muscle mass to run twenty-six miles, nor the training—no one ever before told you how to run twenty-six miles. You tried.

You ran your heart out—but you were not prepared for the race.

There is no joy in being so utterly unsuccessful. And there is no reason to be unsuccessful, in running, or in living for Jesus.

Joy comes when we allow the Holy Spirit to work in our lives, giving us the power to live by the guidelines and commandments God has provided in His Word. With the Spirit's power and with the proper training, we can run the race for Jesus like world-class marathoners—victoriously and triumphantly.

God has provided the tools. Knowing that, we can look with confidence at some of the guidelines He has given us to help us live for Him.

General guidelines for Christian living

To begin, we need to grasp some of the biblical teachings that lay a basic foundation for daily living. Like the fundamentals in a sport, these guidelines show us how to establish a basic game plan for life—one that we can build on with later principles that are more spiritual in nature. But keep in mind as we talk about these concepts that we cannot do these things on our own. We need the power of the Holy Spirit in us.

Be willing to work

"If a man will not work, he shall not eat" (2 Thessalonians 3:10).

God honors the worker. Even before Adam and Eve sinned and caused the disastrous fall that left us all sinners, they were workers. In the garden paradise they called home, they did work that God gave them to do in their perfect environment. By giving

Adam the responsibility of tending the animals, God showed that work is honorable and profitable—not a curse that has been dumped on us because of sin.

The New Testament also affirms the value of work with verses such as Ephesians 4:28, which says, "He who has been stealing must steal no longer, but must work, doing something useful with his own hands, that he may have something to share with those in need." Work is honorable because it not only meets the needs of the family, but it also provides for those who cannot work. Our labors are part of the system God created to sustain civilization. It is our responsibility to do our share of the work.

Be calm and trust God

"Do not be anxious about anything, but . . . present your requests to God" (Philippians 4:6).

"Relax, you've got Master Card." So said the advertising campaign. It's hard to relax, though, when every day that goes by adds another double-digit interest amount to your balance.

If you watch much TV, you are aware of the many products available to help you relax. There are so many things out there to relax you that it seems the only thing you have to watch out for is that infernal pink bunny marching around drumming up business for batteries.

Yet we are not calm. There is a restlessness among people in this society, and it cannot be treated with sleeping pills or soft music or the latest money-saving plan. There is a fear in our society—one so strong that you can almost reach out and touch it.

Do you feel this restlessness? This uneasiness

that comes from living face-to-face with an uncertain future? This nervousness that comes from having problems you can't seem to lick?

This restlessness blocks our happiness by dropping before us a curtain of doubt and fear. Instead of seeing the hand of God in everything and feeling the love of God reassuring us, we see the curtain that screens God out by coming between us and Him with burdens too great for us to bear.

The world we live in can never tell us how to relax. It can never give us a calmness of the soul. It's not easy to be calm in a world with more problems than sensible solutions. The only source of true peace is total, complete faith and dependence on God's goodness and love. We can relax only as we put our lives in God's hands, trusting that our needs will be met and that our troubles are much better handled by Him than by us.

Be content with God's provisions

"Be content with what you have" (Hebrews 13:5).

One of the most dangerous teachings you might come across within the Christian community is what is sometimes called "prosperity doctrine."

This philosophy says that God does not want anyone to be poor or struggling so if you have enough faith (and often if you donate to the right organizations), God will pour out His blessings on you.

Yet Scripture is very clear that God expects us to seek contentment, not riches. It's true that some Christians do receive monetary blessings that go far beyond anything most of us ever experience. However, the expectation that God will provide such rewards to each of us is not biblically grounded.

Rather, God expects us to learn how to live with whatever circumstances He allows us to experience.

A prime example is the apostle Paul. We often call him the greatest apostle or the greatest of the New Testament writers or the greatest missionary. He was, without a doubt, a man who loved Jesus Christ and trusted God to a degree many of us will never achieve. His faith was a model for us to emulate.

But Paul was far from being a coddled, chauffeured, pampered, high-bank-account Christian. Instead, he lived almost a hand-to-mouth existence as a missionary. He worked a side job sewing tents to support his full-time ministry. He spent long, dreary nights in jails that would make modern-day prisons look like the Sheraton. He was shipwrecked, beaten, and booted out of town.

Yet he was the one who wrote these words of testimony to the people of Philippi: "I have learned to be content whatever the circumstances" (Philippians 4:11).

And it was he who told young Timothy, "Godliness with contentment is great gain" (1 Timothy 6:6).

What makes our lives rich and full is a godly lifestyle marked by a spirit of contentment with what God has provided. This contentment is not easy to achieve if we depend on our own resources and look around at what others have. But it is attainable if we dedicate ourselves to trusting God's Holy Spirit to lift us up and empower us no matter what our circumstances. God does not only ask us to be content, but He also provides a Helper to make it happen.

Live totally for God

"Whatever you do, do it all for the glory of God" (1 Corinthians 10:31).

One thing sets the Christian life apart from most other religious experiences that you may hear about. Christianity is a twenty-four-hour-a-day faith.

Perhaps you're familiar with people who attend a church service on Sunday and seem to enjoy the religious experience of this once-a-week chance to get in touch with God. Yet when you see them on Tuesday, absolutely nothing in their lives indicates that they even know who God is. They give 167 hours a week to self and 1 hour a week to God.

Maybe you experienced that kind of life before the Holy Spirit worked in your life and you accepted Jesus' gift of salvation.

As you venture into the previously unknown world of being a Christian, it is vital to realize that every minute of every day belongs to God. As you adopt an attitude of constantly doing everything for God's glory, you will discover that your faith affects many areas of life that people do not normally think of as religious.

> • Our faith can affect how we drive our cars, for even that is a testimony of our Christlikeness.
> • Our faith can affect how we handle our jobs, for we are not working for God's glory if we are lazy.
> • Our faith can affect our relationships, for God is not glorified if we are vindictive or hold grudges or are untruthful.
> • Our faith can affect how we interact with our neighbors, for we know that we need to reflect

Christ's love to them even when their dog decides to dig up our azaleas.

When we make a conscious effort to allow God's Spirit to direct our thinking and actions so that we show the glory of God in every act of every day, we cannot help but improve our personality, increase our productivity, enhance our friendships, and impress our neighbors. We can't help but be different, better people.

Guidelines for honoring God

God is jealous of our affections. He created us for His glory, He provided us with a world of beauty and opportunity, He sacrificed His Son for us, and He gave us His very Spirit as our guide. So it is no surprise that He expects us to honor Him.

Because we love God and want to demonstrate our appreciation for our salvation, we will want to pay homage to Him with our lives. But how do we do it?

Some religions suggest that honoring God consists of elaborate rituals or painful tasks. Others suggest self-denying actions such as offering sacrifices or making pilgrimages. But how different those activities are from what God expects of us! He doesn't want us to perform needless rites; they have no saving power. What He does want is our heartfelt, uninhibited love. When we love God, we automatically depend on His Spirit to help us practice disciplines of life and mind that lead to an entire lifestyle and attitude that centers on Him.

Let's look at some of the guidelines for how we honor God and see how we can incorporate them into our lives.

Pursue Christ

"Grow in the grace and knowledge of our Lord and Savior Jesus Christ" (2 Peter 3:18).

What is grace, and how can we grow in it? Michael Green, English clergyman and author, has described grace as "God's incredible generosity in strengthening us although we don't deserve it."

I think I know a little about grace from dealing with my son. If ever there was a perpetual motion machine in jeans, it is Steven. And occasionally his energy gets him into trouble because his body performs before his mind informs. Like when he broke the lamp in the family room, causing a mini-fireworks display. At that point in his existence, Steven needed grace. He deserved perhaps a few minutes of uninterrupted contemplation in a quiet corner of his bedroom, but I decided not to make a big deal about the lamp. It was repairable, and he had not meant any malice. He was just trying to screw on the lampshade and got carried away.

Anyway, I fixed the lamp and let it go at that. For this time at least, Steven was spared punishment, he benefited from my grace, and, as we talked about how to fix the lamp, he learned an additional lesson.

God deals with us that way all the time. His grace is ours for the taking, because the penalty for our sin has been paid. But that is just the start. As we continue to pursue Christ in our lives—as we grow more and more like Him—we demonstrate the grace Jesus demonstrated best through salvation. As Paul reminds us, "it is by grace you have been saved" (Ephesians 2:5, 8), and it is by growth in grace that we show to others the result of that salvation.

Abandon yourself to God

"Offer your bodies as living sacrifices, holy and pleasing to God" (Romans 12:1).

When I played college basketball, I made a conscious decision each fall to walk into that gym and indicate to my coach that I was completely at his disposal.

It would not have benefited my team to report to practice and announce, "Hey, Coach! Here I am. I want to shoot baskets and dribble the ball, but don't ask me to run laps, play defense, or get all sweaty."

I would have been out of there faster than you can say, "Full court press." No, I had to present myself, in essence, as a living sacrifice. Whatever he asked me to do for the good of the team, I agreed to do.

As Christians, our responsibility is to do the same thing. We need to say to our creator-God, our Savior and Lord, "Here I am. Whatever You want me to do, I am willing to do it."

The comforting thing to keep in mind as we consider giving ourselves completely and without reservation to God for His use is that He will not call on us to do something for which He has not already equipped us. Later in Romans, the apostle Paul explains that "we have different gifts, according to the grace given us" (12:6). So what we have to do as new believers is discover how God has uniquely gifted us to serve Him. That's something we will discuss in a later chapter.

Knowing clearly the task ahead we can then abandon ourselves to God, strengthened by the knowledge that He created us specifically to do this effort for Him.

Seek a change for the better

"Do not conform any longer to the pattern of this world, but be transformed by the renewing of your mind" (Romans 12:2).

Some people hide their faith really well. They come to a crisis in their lives, and they hear the gospel. So, thinking this is the answer and solution to all their problems, they accept Jesus as their Savior. But you never see any evidence of it. They retain a sour expression, they refuse to make any changes in their lifestyle, and they blend in with the unsaved people in the world just as they did before.

That isn't the way this thing called salvation, and the resulting sanctification, is supposed to work.

A good example of how it works is Greg Buchanan. If you are looking for some interesting music to enhance your spiritual life, try his. Don't be put off by the fact that he plays the harp. Listen anyway. His rare style of plucking and strumming produces a toe-tapping worship experience that you never thought you'd hear from a harpist.

Anyway, the reason I mention him is that he is a good example of how Romans 12:2 works. Before he accepted Jesus as his Savior, Greg blended perfectly into the contemporary way of life. He was a heavy drinker. He was a drug user. He was a womanizer. He played his harp in all the smoke-filled night spots he could haul the thing into.

Then he heard the gospel and was saved.

Within months, he stopped conforming to the pattern of this world, and he was transformed. He changed from a hard-driving, alcohol-swigging, miserable druggie to a sober, God-praising, joyful Christian. He took the first and most important step of accepting Jesus as his Savior, but he didn't stop there. He sought a change for the better by renewing his mind with Scripture and Christian fellowship. Today he stands out from the world in sharp contrast, and his testimony is as beautiful as his harp music.

The transaction that saved us made us a new creation in Christ (2 Corinthians 5:17) and caused us to be sanctified, or set apart (1 Corinthians 6:11), in God's eyes. But it didn't make us perfect. Therefore we must, as Greg Buchanan did and as Romans 12:2 describes, decide to stop letting the world mold our thinking. We must consciously, with God's help, be changed into something better.

Let the Holy Spirit be your guide

"Since we live by the Spirit, let us keep in step with the Spirit" (Galatians 5:25).

Do you remember those frightening times when you were a child and some kind of danger seemed loomingly close? Perhaps you were alone in your darkened room and your mind was busy conjuring up thoughts of all kinds of monsters lurking under your bed. Or maybe thunder rumbled and lightning flashed, and you didn't like either of them. What did you do? You called out to Mom or Dad. You wanted to know that they were close by. Their presence was all you needed to calm your fears.

Life can sometimes seem like a stormy night with dangers crashing and flashing around us, threatening to darken our joy. As a Christian, you now have the presence of One who is a compassionate Father. You can call out to the Holy Spirit to calm

your heart and assist you when the going gets
rough.

Jesus knew that the early Christians would
need the presence of the Holy Spirit. In fact, He indicated to them that they should not begin the mission
He had designed for them until they had received the
Holy Spirit (Acts 1:8). He knew the difficulty of the
task, and He knew they could not overcome the fears
and struggles they would face as witnesses for
Christ without the help of the Spirit living in them.
The same is true of us.

To benefit from the presence of the Spirit, we
can heed the advice of three verses from the pen of
Paul.

First, we should "be filled with the Spirit" (Ephesians 5:18). Paul contrasted being filled with the
Spirit with the inebriation of a drunkard, indicating
that we need to be under God's control. Just as we
can see the effect of wine on a drunkard by his or her
outward behavior, we can see the effect of the Spirit
on a Christian by seeing if he or she displays the
fruit detailed in Galatians 5:22-23.

Second, we must be careful not to "grieve the
Holy Spirit" (Ephesians 4:30). The Holy Spirit is, as
we learned earlier, personal, and has feelings that
can be grieved. We should treat Him and His presence with respect, careful not to let "unwholesome
talk" (Ephesians 5:29) or "bitterness, rage and anger, brawling and slander, along with every form of
malice" (5:31) characterize our lives.

A third responsibility we have toward the Spirit
who strengthens us and lifts us up out of fearfulness
is to "keep in step" with Him (Galatians 5:25). We do
that when we let the characteristics of love, peace,

patience, kindness, goodness, faithfulness, gentleness, and self-control mark our lives. We are out of step with the Spirit when we act in any other way. And when we are out of step with the Spirit, we not only grieve Him but we also cause ourselves a lot of unnecessary trouble.

Value the teaching of the Bible

"Like newborn babies, crave pure spiritual milk, so that by it you may grow up in your salvation" (1 Peter 2:2).

You are what you eat. Or at least that's how the saying goes. While that may be debatable when it comes to food, it is absolutely true in spiritual things. You can grow no faster spiritually than your intake of the Word of God allows.

That is not to say that you have to gorge yourself by locking yourself in a room until you've read the whole Bible. Many people who do not even own a completed version of the Bible have grown faster than those of us with enough Bibles to stock a library. In countries where access to the Bible is restricted, Scripture can become so precious to believers that they think about it continually. Meditating on the few shreds of God's truth that are available to them, they have grown because they are completing the communication link with God: God to man through His Word; man to God through prayer.

One of the advantages of having the Holy Spirit living within us and influencing our lives is that He plants within us the drive to know God better. We know that has happened when we desire the milk of the Word. At that point in our spiritual journey, we are like the student who has gone beyond the stage of learning only in order to get a passing grade; we have graduated to the point where we learn about God through His Word because of a burning desire to know Him better. We begin to value the teaching of the Bible because we recognize that it is the only way we get to know God intimately.

Misconceptions about the Christian life

Whenever anything good happens, it seems, someone concocts an evil twin as its counterpart. It happens in the Christian life when a teacher begins to go beyond the basic teachings of Scripture and starts adding new qualifications, standards, and rules to what is expected. Following are several examples of false guidelines for Christian living.

Christian living as legalism

You cannot do better than to try to live each day according to biblical guidelines. Never will you go wrong if you try to please God by obeying His Word, serving Him, and helping others. However, you can go wrong if you see your goodness as a reason for pride—or as a means of acceptance before God.

Living for the Lord according to the guidelines of the Bible is an act of the heart—one that flows from love for God. The Christian life is not like the Scouts, in which you do tasks out of obligation in an attempt to earn merit badges. Any act of service or obedience done through obligation or self-centered motives is an act of legalism, not an act of love for God.

Christian living as a checklist

As we saw in chapter 1, the Pharisees lived by the

checklist. They had their roster of right and wrong activities, and if they felt they were following it to the letter, they felt they were godly.

If we live by a list, figuring that if we don't do these ten things and that if we do these other ten things we are pleasing God, we have missed the point. Sure there are right and wrong things to do, but godliness comes when we maintain a strong relationship with God, not when we coldly follow a list. When our relationship with God is strong, the Holy Spirit will help us avoid certain actions and guide us to participate in others, but the relationship and being in tune with the Spirit must come first.

Christian living as a spectator sport

Sitting in a pew is an admirable thing to do, but it is not the ultimate Christian exercise. We can easily be lulled into a false sense of satisfaction if we think that our responsibilities to God are fulfilled because we put in our time at church listening to a sermon and singing the hymns. The same is true of tuning in to Christian radio, putting sermon tapes in our Walkman, or reading good Christian books. These should all be stimulants to action, not ends in themselves. The measure of our lives as Christians is not what kind of spectators at Christian events we are. We need to put our faith into action personally.

Christian living as following a person or a movement

Only one Person is infallible, and His name is Jesus. Recently I heard a writer who had spent several months uncovering a rather sinister and not very Christlike side of a man who was considered a

Christian celebrity. One of the most frustrating exchanges he had was with a woman who called the writer and berated him for what he had discovered. She was a follower of the celebrity's teachings and she did not like the fact that the writer had revealed some negative things about this man. Instead of believing the carefully documented truth, she chose to believe what she wanted to believe.

It is not hard to be caught up in this kind of thinking. To avoid it, remember that our only guide for faith and practice is the Bible, and if someone suggests otherwise, that individual is digging a grave of deceit that may bury many.

Living by the guidelines that God has so graciously provided for us in His Word should never be tedious chore. It is a privilege and an honor to be chosen to live the right way—the way God designed us to live. Entrusting our lives to the principles of Scripture should always arouse in us a feeling of gratitude to God for not leaving us to fend for ourselves in a world of bewildering and confusing information. All about us we see people wandering as through a maze, seemingly without a clue how to live. How encouraging to know that the One who made us told us how we should live and gave us help in the form of the Holy Spirit to make sure it can happen!

Getting into the Word
What specific guidelines can you establish by using these verses?
- Matthew 5:24
- Matthew 10:16
- Matthew 22:37, 39

- Romans 12:2
- Romans 12:16
- 1 Corinthians 15:58
- Ephesians 6:4
- Colossians 3:15
- 1 Timothy 4:12
- 2 Timothy 2:24
- Hebrews 13:5
- Hebrews 10:35
- 2 Peter 3:18

Thinking it through

Consider the following questions as you reflect on what you have read in this chapter.

- What might happen to you if you should decide not to live by the guidelines God has clearly spelled out?
- What biblical occurrences show what happens to people who do not live according to the guidelines God established?
- What advantages can you see to living by God's standards?
- Are any of the guidelines mentioned in this chapter troublesome to you? How can you make sure you are doing what honors God in those troublesome areas?

Getting practical

Try these suggestions for applying what you have read.

- Write down what your philosophy for living was before you accepted Jesus. Explain how that has changed after reading about God's guidelines.

• In a notebook, write down specific times that living by God's guidelines has helped make life go better for you. Also note any times they have made things more complicated. What conclusions can you come to?

Exploring the subject further

These books can be helpful resources as you work on putting God's standards into practice in your own life.

• *Beating Mediocrity: Six Habits of the Highly Effective Christian,* John Guest
• *First Things First,* Roger C. Palms
• *What Jesus Said About Successful Living,* Haddon Robinson
• *Spiritual Disciplines for Ordinary People,* Keith Drury

8

A Life of No Regrets

How do I know what is right and what is wrong?

To a writer, a computer is the best thing since the eraser.

Yet when I first was introduced to the possibility of writing and editing on a keyboard while the words appeared on a TV screen in front of me, I was about as enthusiastic as a dog facing a bath. I had depended on my trusty yellow legal pad for a long time, and I didn't want to give it up.

That first brush with a computer happened quite a few years ago, and I quickly got over my lack of enthusiasm. Now I couldn't bear the thought of writing a book, or even a long article, without my Macintosh computer. I am definitely a computer convert.

Something new entered my life, though, when I accepted the computer as my desktop friend.

A book.

It's called the Macintosh Reference, and it's no small accomplishment. The thing has more than 400 pages in it, and much of it is written in language that is unfamiliar to me. When I first got my Mac, I

didn't know the difference between a mouse and a
RAM, and the Macintosh Reference was not my idea
of a good read.

One thing I noticed, though, as I leafed through
this ponderous work, was that it not only told me
what I was supposed to do to make sure my computer and I remained on speaking terms, but it also told
me clearly that were things I should absolutely not
do if I wanted to be a successful Mac-er.

Now, a lot of people don't like someone or some
book telling them what to do. They think it cramps
their style or somehow hinders their creativity or
freedom. "I can decide for myself, thank you, about
how I run my computer," such a person might say.

That kind of thinking can cause a person with a
personal computer a lot of problems. For instance, if
I am typing merrily along on my keyboard and don't
realize that I'm supposed to save my document before turning off the computer, I can wipe out hours
of work with one flick of a switch. I may not like someone telling me how to run my computer, but if I don't
obey the warnings, life can get pretty miserable.

Page 167 of my Macintosh Reference gives me a
few more warnings:

•Never move a Macintosh when the hard disk
drive is operating.

•Do not place the computer on its side unless it
is designed to operate this way.

•Avoid spilling any liquids on or near the drive.
And other pages throughout the book tell me
things like:

•Be sure that any disk you plan to initialize contains no information you want to save, because
you'll lose that information during initialization.

Now, I have a choice when I see these warnings. I can pay attention to them because I know that the people who wrote the manual want me to be successful in my work with the Mac, or I could throw the book in the trash and figure things out for myself.

I have learned through experience, though, that anything that jeopardizes all the data I have placed on my computer is my mortal enemy. For instance, I know that if I stick an important disk in my computer—one with a book manuscript on it, for instance—and a message comes up asking if I want the disk initialized, I had better know how to respond. I need to know what is the right thing to do, according to the book. Guesswork could have me staring at pages and pages of blank screen where pages and pages of my book used to be. My coexistence with my computer would be a story of one sad regret after another if I ignored the guidelines set down by the folks who created the computer I use and who know more about it than I can ever hope to learn.

Life can be much like operating a computer. You can live it by trial and error while ignoring the owner's manual, or you can take every precaution possible to make sure you're running things the way the Designer wants you to do. The result of that choice will dictate the course your life takes.

The Bible is that owner's manual. It, like my Macintosh Reference, is rather large, and it contains some warnings to protect us. We can look at God's warnings as helpful, or we can look at them as irritating. As I do with my Mac suggestions, I hope you decide to look at God's guidance in Scripture as insurance against wrecking something very important.

Deadly consequences

We need only to look around at our world to realize what happens when people live without obeying the warnings from God's Word.

For instance, there is no question what Scripture says about honesty, lying, and misrepresentation. The Bible points out that dishonesty is wrong and that it leads only to trouble (see Proverbs 12:22; 22:6). Look at the difficulties people get into in all walks of life when they are dishonest. From Wall Street traders to S & L presidents to people who cheat on their income taxes, they discover that living a lie always lands them in big trouble. Whether they are cheating on the floor of the stock exchange or scamming people to invest in swampland or lying about their income, they can't escape the destruction that always comes to those who defy God's principles.

With those modern-day examples in mind, let's look at a couple of Bible-era people whose choices made it difficult for them to please God. Perhaps if we understand their stories, we can see how our choices directly affect what happens to us.

One of the Bible's early episodes concerns two brothers: Cain and Abel. Sons of Adam and Eve, they grew up to be farmers. When Cain's crops came in, he brought "some of the fruits of the soil as an offering to the Lord" (Genesis 4:3). Abel, on the other hand, "brought fat portions from some of the firstborn of his flock" (4:4). The difference was in their desire to please God. Cain was somewhat lax in his offering, while Abel was sincere and dedicated. Cain brought what was convenient to bring; Abel brought the best.

One did what was right, and he did it with a good attitude. The other tried to get by with as little effort as possible. And God's response to the two young men can help us see how important it is to do what He wants.

Cain's gift was not accepted by God. He knew that Cain was going through the motions and that neither his heart nor his gift were right. As a result, God told him, "If you do what is right, will you not be accepted? But if you do not do what is right, sin is crouching at your door" (4:7).

Apparently the sin lying in wait for Cain was murder, for we see that he was so angry with his brother for bringing an acceptable offering that he killed him.

Cain's first choice, to bring an inappropriate offering and give it in an unacceptable way, was wrong. And that led him to a much more serious sin. His failure to please God led to his fall from son of Adam to murderer of Abel.

In the book of Acts we read of an astounding incident that demonstrates the importance of truthfulness. A man named Ananias got involved in the local church fund drive. Actually what was happening was that the people in the local church were bringing gifts to help the church and its ministries. Many people were giving all their possessions to the church.

Then along came Ananias. He and his wife had just come into some money through the sale of a piece of land. Together they decided that they would just bring part of the proceeds to give to the church, not the whole thing. When they brought the money and put it at the apostles' feet, Peter immediately knew that something was wrong.

He confronted Ananias and asked him how he could have lied to the Holy Spirit. We don't have all the details, but apparently Ananias had agreed to bring everything, but had "kept back part of the money for himself" (Acts 5:2). Peter told him, "You have lied not to men but to God" (5:4).

First he lied, then he died. Dropped dead on the spot.

Three hours later his wife was asked to verify the amount they had received from selling the land, that they had indeed sold the land for the amount of money that was being given. When she lied and said they had, she too fell down and breathed her last.

Now, this could get real scary. Here you are, a new Christian or one who is looking anew to live for God, and you read a story like this. Does this mean that you'll die if you don't follow the clear right and wrong guidelines God has provided for his people in the Bible?

Certainly not. But many people are dying because they refuse to follow scriptural guidelines for lifestyle decisions. When we see the toll exacted by sexually transmitted diseases, by vengeful hatred exploding into violence, or by substance abuse of various kinds, we would be foolish not to follow guidelines that have worked for thousands of years.

Godly standards

As we look at the following principles for understanding how to know what's right, remember that God's love is the motivation behind any restrictions He has given us and that His Holy Spirit is the source for power that can help us obey. If any of these standards contradicts a lifestyle that was yours before you became a Christian, remember that God gives us such standards to guarantee our joy and to protect us—not to be a big killjoy. The One who can see the end from the beginning has clearly told us how to avoid a life of regrets.

Watch out for sin

"Avoid every kind of evil" (1 Thessalonians 5:22).

Suppose you go to the doctor for a checkup. A few days later she has all the results in, so she calls you into her office and tells you that you have an unbelievably high cholesterol level. She thinks that the best thing you can do to avoid clogging up your arteries any further is to stay away from foods with fat in them.

You know she's a reputable doctor, you trust her word, and you're sure she knows what's good for you. And you really want to avoid a heart attack. So on the way home, you stop at Baskin-Robbins to see if you can resist the ice cream. Then you hit the neighborhood fast food shop to see if your will power can outweigh your desire for a Big Mac and a large order of fries. Finally, you pick up an extra dozen eggs at the market, just to prove you can resist a ready supply of cholesterol around the house.

Absurd? Of course! But it is not so different from what we sometimes do to ourselves spiritually. We are sure that God is good, we believe that His Word is true, and we are confident that He wants what's best for us when He says, "Avoid every kind of evil." Yet we think we can flirt with evil and not have it damage us. Instead of avoiding those places where evil lurks, we get as close to them as we can.

To "avoid every kind of evil," for instance, we
need to make a conscious effort to make sure our TV
and other viewing habits don't become avenues for
introducing sin into our homes. Whenever possible,
we must avoid conversations that dishonor our
Lord. We need to walk away from situations that
may lead to unfaithfulness to a spouse, dishonesty
in handling money, or deceit in business practices.

We don't have to become hermits, but we do
need to be careful to avoid the evil that is so much a
part of life in our society.

Watch what you think
"Abstain from sinful desires" (1 Peter 2:11).

Even when one is careful to practice the right
outward actions, it is easy to slip into a mental world
where one indulges in imaginary evils.

This is what Joni Eareckson Tada did after she
suffered a paralyzing diving accident in her youth.
Suddenly bedridden and unable to move, she could
not sin with her body. There was no way she could
steal or drive a car too fast or fool around with a boy-
friend. So she began to conjure up sins in her mind.
In her book Joni, she tells that she finally had to
come face-to-face with the fact that her mental sins
were as bad as anything she could have done as an
able-bodied person.

The God who created us knows that even after
we are redeemed and made part of the family of God,
we have the capability of putting on a false front. We
can make it appear to others that we are living right
while having thought lives full of sinful desires.

The problem with sinful desires is that they
seem to have a slimy little life of their own. Using

terms that paint a picture of abduction, the apostle James spells out the pattern that can develop: "Each one is tempted when, by his own evil desire, he is dragged away and enticed. Then, after desire has conceived, it gives birth to sin . . ." (James 1:14–15). No wonder Peter said we should not allow sinful desires to occupy our minds. They can kidnap us and hold us hostage if we don't watch out.

Keep your mind clear

"Do not get drunk on wine" (Ephesians 5:18).

Among Christians, you can easily find people on both sides of the issue of drinking. Some will tell you that the Bible does not prohibit all drinking, just drunkenness. They will point to a verse that Paul wrote to Timothy, which says, "Stop drinking only water, and use a little wine because of your stomach" (1 Timothy 5:23).

Other believers will embrace a position that supports complete abstinence from alcohol. They will point to a verse such as Proverbs 20:1, which says, "Wine is a mocker and beer is a brawler; whoever is led astray by them is not wise." This seeming contradiction of supporting evidence from both sides of the issue could make it difficult for the new or searching Christian to decide what is best.

This question is one of those dilemmas that cannot be answered specifically with chapter and verse. However you choose, I recommend these biblical principles as a guide to making the safest, and I think most God-honoring, choice. Let's start with Ephesians 5:18. Here Paul is talking about the elements in your life that can control you. The choice he presents is between being controlled by an outside agent, in this case alcohol, or being controlled by an inner entity—the Holy Spirit. Look at the contrast. One may lead to debauchery or corruption. The other leads to closeness to God.

Although Paul's emphasis is on making sure that we allow the Holy Spirit to control our lives (which, as we saw earlier, is the key to godly living), he makes a good argument against alcohol. Alcohol may rob one of the chance to control one's thinking or of the ability to let the Holy Spirit control. The negative effect of alcohol on behavior is a clear warning that, if we want to keep our minds clear and useful to God, alcohol is not a substance that we should favor.

Fight off evil forces

"Do not give the devil a foothold" (Ephesians 4:27). "Resist the devil, and he will flee from you" (James 4:7).

It's a war out there. We are in a deadly battle with the fiercest enemy humanity has ever known. He is the archenemy of God—a fallen angel who set out at the beginning of creation to usurp God's position as head of the universe. His name is Satan, and he takes up his battle one person at a time.

That means he is out to get you.

But God has given us some clear guidelines for fighting off the devil and his evil forces.

First, it is vital that we not give Satan any advantages in his attacks against us. Think of a tug-of-war. In a tug-of-war, one of the best strategies is for a team to dig itself a deep foothold. The apostle Paul says, "Do not give the devil a foothold." He is referring to anger and grudges, which are sure footholds for Satan in destroying personal relationships.

But we can easily think of other footholds that we allow the devil to dig in our lives, making the battle much more difficult for us. We let Satan dig in against us any time we allow jealousy, envy, immorality, dishonesty, or a myriad of other sins to establish themselves in our lives. That is why when we discover one of these problems we must get rid of it immediately. We can never succeed in our quest for a right relationship with Christ if we give Satan these opportunities to yank us around.

If you're looking for a way to avoid that, look at James 4:7. Satan, for all his power and his blustering about how he is going to knock God off the throne, can be thwarted. It takes two steps to keep him away and to avoid letting him get a foothold.

Our initial responsibility is to submit to God.

Our second responsibility to avoid letting Satan tug away at us is to resist him. We have to put up a fight. We aren't to be like the convenience store workers who are told not to resist if someone comes in to rob the cash register. We are not helpless clerks facing down a sawed-off shotgun; we have the most powerful force in the world behind us. We are sons and daughters of the King of kings, and our Father has equipped us with the Holy Spirit to help us do battle. To stay tapped in to that power source, James tells us, we must submit to God (James 4:7). This means we trust His Word when it tells us that certain actions are good for us and others are bad. This is not easy, but if we maintain a close relationship with God, talking with Him and continually checking His teachings, we will find submission to Him to be a possible mission. And we will be able to stand our ground and fight. And notice what happens when we do. James says Satan turns tail and runs. "He will flee from you."

You do not have to fear the evil forces around you. You are on the winning side.

Protect yourself

"Put on the full armor of God so that you can take your stand against the devil's schemes" (Ephesians 6:11).

This thing called the Christian life would be a bit easier if there were always a clear line separating what is right from what is wrong. But Satan is too sly to let that happen. He is the world's number one liar and deceiver, and he likes nothing better than blurring the distinctions between right and wrong. The apostle Paul called these tricks "the devil's schemes."

So how do we protect ourselves against the devil's schemes?

It's a matter of equipment. Just as a worker in a nuclear plant would never even think of getting close to radioactive materials without first putting on every piece of protective gear he has available, so we should not dare going out into a Satan-active world without our "full armor of God" (described in Ephesians 6:14–17). It is the only way we can "stand firm" and resist Satan completely. Let's look at the armor we are to put on before we go out to battle the schemer.

  • Belt of truth—God is Truth. All that we say must correspond to the truthfulness that should characterize God's children.
  • Breastplate of righteousness—We will always live with God's approval and Satan's disapproval when we do what is right.

• Gospel of peace covering the feet—We should go about diligently sharing the gospel that gives inner peace through faith in Christ.

• Shield of faith—Satan will aim some sharp attacks at us, but our faith in Christ will deflect those arrows.

• Helmet of salvation—The knowledge of your relationship with God can help you when Satan attacks.

• Sword of the Spirit, which is the word of God— As with so much of the Christian life, it is the Word of God that gives us the ammunition to attack those who stand against us.

With our armor in place, we are ready to step out into a world where Satan tries to confuse us about right and wrong.

There will be times when the people you know, work with, or are related to will wonder about your newfound interest in living a life that is pure and good. There is little popular call in our society for people to live by guidelines higher and more noble than the ones we see advocated on television, in the movies, and in the private lives of some of our public officials. Yet it can never be wrong for us to look past the small discomfort that a stand for godly living may cause us. It can never harm us to gauge our lives by an unchangeable standard that has been around for thousands of years and that was given by the God who designed us and knows what makes us work best. Remember, no one or no institution loves you, cares for you, or wants the best for you like He does. Trust His guidance. And live for Him. It will take your relationship with Him to new heights, and it will protect you from a world of trouble and regret.

Getting into the Word

What specific guidelines can you discover from these verses?
- Romans 6:12
- Romans 12:2
- Romans 14:13
- 1 Corinthians 15:33
- 2 Corinthians 6:17
- Ephesians 5:11
- 1 Thessalonians 5:22
- 1 Peter 2:11
- 1 Peter 2:1

Thinking it through

Consider the following questions as you reflect on what you have read in this chapter.

- What have you been doing recently that you know does not please the Lord nor enhance your relationship with Him? What should you do about it? Is there a passage of Scripture you can turn to when you keep running into such problems?
- How can you be sure that your salvation does not depend on your living by God's standards for behavior?
- How can you answer people (maybe yourself sometimes) who say, "All God wants to do is take away your fun by making you follow all those rules"?
- Who are some mature Christians you respect because of their lifestyle and their evident love for Jesus? What can you learn from them?

• What happens when you blow it and fall back into some sin or even venture into a new one? What does 1 John 1:9 say to you then?

Getting practical

Try these suggestions for applying what you have read.

• Read Romans 12 and take some notes on what it says to you about living as a Christian in a hateful, prideful world.

• Write a short letter to a fictional friend, explaining why an activity that this friend is suggesting is now off-limits to you because of your relation with Jesus Christ.

• Watch a prime-time TV program and write down the situations, words, or characterizations that seem to go against what you think God's standards are.

• Use a concordance to find all the passages that use the word *temptation* in the Bible. Read those passages to find out what role temptation plays in the problem of sin.

Exploring the subject further

If you'd like to read more about God's guidelines and resisting sin, consider these books.

• *There I Go Again*, Steven R. Mosley
• *Private Obsessions*, Lee Ezell
• *Why Christians Sin*, J. Kirk Johnston

9

An Opportunity to Help

How can I serve in the church?

There's nothing quite like that first week on a new job.

You made it past the stone-faced personnel director, and you somehow impressed the people who are paid to figure you out via those psychologically demanding questions. You've read the employee handbook, and you remember almost none of it. You show up early the first day. And you stand around a lot.

Because you don't know anybody, you feel a bit ill at ease. And because you don't know anything about where stuff goes or what to say to people, you spend large portions of the day trying to look invisible. No one really trusts you to do anything yet, so your workload is smaller than your ego. It's an uncomfortable situation because you understand that you are getting paid, but you don't think you are doing anything to help.

A few weeks pass, and you make it through your probation period. You can throw away that button that says, "Trainee," and you begin to feel good about going to work. You feel like you're contributing, and when you get your paycheck every couple of weeks or so, you don't feel like you're stealing the company's money. You have arrived as a valuable employee and an asset to the people you work for. You are doing something worthwhile.

New Christians can sometimes feel like new employees. They show up at church and they notice that other people are busy doing things. Everyone is walking purposefully, rushing from this room to the next, having important hallway conversations, and getting their names in the church bulletin under headings like "Serving in the nursery today" or "At the piano today" or "High School Chat and Chew at the Smedley's."

You have the feeling you ought to be getting involved, too. You know that as a Christian you have been promised all kinds of spiritual rewards, and you feel you ought to do something worthwhile in return. You feel that you ought to be earning your keep. You'd like an opportunity to help.

If you do feel that way, and if you want to get involved, you are definitely on the right track. Considering that the task which faces the church (which means all of God's people put together, not just the people who worship in the same building you worship in) is huge, your help is needed.

As a new "employee," you need to know what the mission of the church is. Just as a company that might hire you has a purpose statement, so does the company of believers have a statement of purpose. The job of the church is to "go and make disciples of all nations, baptizing them in the name of the Father and of the Son and of the Holy Spirit, teaching them to obey everything I have commanded you" (Matthew 28:19–20). There are two parts to this purpose statement: first, people have to be led to a saving knowledge of Jesus Christ and, second, they need to be taught Christian faith.

The task of any helper in this endeavor, then, is to help people see their need for a Savior or to help believers to grow, or both. What is exciting about this effort and your part in it is that God has equipped you in a special way to do a particular job.

Ideally, an employer wants to place people in positions for which they are trained. If you went to school to learn to be a computer programmer, a company would not want to start you down a employment track that would lead to becoming a side-order chef. You would be frustrated, and the company would be wasting your skills.

God has taken this idea of matching skills and jobs one step further. He Himself has created in each of us specific abilities He wants us to use to serve Him. Our efforts at the beginning of our "employment" as believers should be to discover what skills we were given and how those skills can best be used in the work of the church.

A part of the whole

Were you ever in a play? Remember how each member in the cast depended completely on every other actor? Even the smallest bit player must come through for the production to work. The play is not a fragmented collection of unrelated parts; it is a unit that is woven together out of dialogue and action. If someone misses a cue or forgets a line, the play unravels. And it doesn't matter if the error is made by the lead or by someone with just six lines. The play just doesn't work quite right without that portion.

God has designed life in the church to be somewhat like that. He has given out the parts, so to speak, so that each Christian has a definite role to fill. If that role is not filled, then the work cannot go on as God planned.

The apostle Paul used a similar analogy: "Just as each of us has one body with many members, and these members do not all have the same function, so in Christ we who are many form one body, and each member belongs to all the others. We have different gifts, according to the grace given us" (Romans 12:4–6). The body of Christ consists of many parts, all with different strengths. Peter explained how we are to use the those strengths when he wrote, "Each one should use whatever gift he has received to serve others, faithfully administering God's grace in its various forms" (1 Peter 4:10).

When we sit in church and look up on the platform at the pastor, it's easy to think that there can't be much more important work than that. Or we hear someone like Steve Green singing gospel music and we figure that God must have handed over to him one of the top jobs among Christians. You think to yourself, Sure, God is going to let me do some work in the church, but I'm so new it can't be anything worth much to anyone.

That may be how it is in many places we work—like at the factory or at the office—but the apostle Paul suggested that things are different for Christians and the work we are to do. Paul wrote, "The body is a unit, though it is made up of many parts; and though all its parts are many, they form one body. So it is with Christ. For we were all baptized by one Spirit into one body—whether Jews or Greeks, slave or free—and we were all given the one Spirit to drink" (1 Corinthians 12:12–13). The work of the whole unit is what is most important, not the status of the individuals who make it up.

Paul went on: "Now the body is not made up of one part but of many. If the foot should say, 'Because I am not a hand, I do not belong to the body,' it would not for that reason cease to be part of the body. And if the ear should say, 'Because I am not an eye, I do not belong to the body,' it would not for that reason cease to be part of the body. If the whole body were an eye, where would the sense of hearing be? If the whole body were an ear, where would the sense of smell be?" (12:14–17). The work that we as Christians are supposed to be doing could not get done if we were all the pastor.

Here's how it works: "But in fact God has arranged the parts in the body, every one of them, just as he wanted them to be. . . . God has combined the members of the body and has given greater honor to the parts that lacked it, so that there should be no division in the body, but that its parts should have equal concern for each other. If one part suffers, every part suffers with it; if one part is honored, every part rejoices with it. Now you are the body of Christ, and each one of you is a part of it" (12:18, 24–27).

Do you feel the encouragement Paul's outline of the work of the church gives to each of us—new or old in the faith? God has put things together just as

He wants them, which means that each of us has a specific job to do. No matter what job we have in working for God, we should receive equal care and concern from those around us. As a unit that God has put together to get His work done, we have a sense of community that helps us cry together, laugh together, and suffer together.

Finding your place in the body

Remembering that each job is important and God-given, we can forget about looking for the job that exalts us and concentrate on finding work that glorifies our Savior and Lord. With that in mind, let's look at some guidelines that can help us pinpoint more specifically what God wants us to do.

Investigate your gift

"If a man's gift is prophesying, let him use it in proportion to his faith. If it is serving, let him serve; if it is teaching, let him teach; if it is encouraging, let him encourage; if it is contributing to the needs of others, let him give generously; if it is leadership, let him govern diligently; if it is showing mercy, let him do it cheerfully" (Romans 12:6–8).

Discovering your spiritual gift may take some help. The list in these verses includes such things as serving, teaching, encouraging, contributing, leading, and showing mercy. It is not an exhaustive list, but it should help us see the wide variety of tasks available.

Perhaps a checklist of things to think about will help.

- What work do you enjoy doing?
- What have you been trained to do?

• What has been a dream of yours to do that you haven't done yet?

• What do you do that people have complimented you about?

• Are you better with people skills, with manual skills, or with mental skills?

• Do you have any hobbies that might be turned into service opportunities?

• Are you more comfortable organizing or being organized?

• What would make you miserable if you had to do it?

• Who are some people who know you well enough to advise you?

Arriving at the right tasks may at first seem a bit like trial and error. It may also take getting to know some people in the church and asking them some questions. But whatever it takes, dive in and give your abilities a try.

At those times when you sit at home with your heart beating hard, wondering if there really is anything for you to do, take comfort in the words of Paul, who spent so much time advising a group of churches full of new believers: "Therefore you do not lack any spiritual gift as you eagerly wait for our Lord Jesus Christ to be revealed" (1 Corinthians 1:7).

Use your gift to build up

"It was he who gave some to be apostles, some to be prophets, some to be evangelists, and some to be pastors and teachers, to prepare God's people for works of service, so that the body of Christ may be built up" (Ephesians 4:11–12).

There is one word that can describe any task that God may appoint us to do: service. When you serve someone, you build him or her up; you don't concern yourself with having your name written on a plaque somewhere.

I know of a woman who typifies this aspect of working in God's kingdom. Her name would be recognized by people in her city and even across the country. Yet without fanfare and without any desire for recognition, she visits a local nursing home to cut the fingernails and toenails of elderly people who can no longer do that.

She serves by building these people up. Her act of caring elevates them in importance from people who might be ignored by society to people who deserve the attention of a fellow Christian who has no lack of things to do with her time. Her gift of mercy and helping, used in this unusual way, challenges us to find places where we can build up other believers.

Use your gift to praise God

"If anyone serves, he should do it with the strength God provides, so that in all things God may be praised through Jesus Christ. To him be the glory and the power for ever and ever. Amen" (1 Peter 4:11).

Whenever a job is done and done well, someone gets praise. A waitress who gets a sizable tip is receiving the praise of a contented diner. A child who gets a Happy Meal at McDonald's for cleaning up her room is getting the praise of a pleased parent.

When it comes to the jobs that we do for God, however, the reward system works differently. If a

Christian does something well and is rewarded for it, the praise needs to be deflected to God. This thought should build in us a deep sense of humility, for we should always be willing to give up the praise for what we do and be willing to transfer it to its rightful object—God. If you see believers who seem to have let their gifts and the resulting praise go to their heads, you can rest assured that they need to incorporate some 1 Peter 4:11 thinking into their lives.

Serve faithfully

"Each one should use whatever gift he has received to serve others, faithfully administering God's grace in its various forms" (1 Peter 4:10).

One of the worst things about the work that goes on in the church is that it is, for the most part, volunteer work. Yet that could also be the best part.

If we look outside of the church, we can see all kinds of organizations that get the job done through volunteer efforts. Whether it is MADD or Right to Life or the parent-teacher organization at school, a majority of the tasks are done by people who don't have to do it, who get paid nothing, and who have about 789 other things to do with their time.

As important as those efforts are, though, none of them can be nearly as vital as the role we have to play in helping God fulfill His purpose statement. Therefore, our faithfulness—our willingness to stick to a job and see it done completely and well—is essential if we really want to pull our weight.

Look for work you can do with confidence

Perhaps you have spent huge amounts of your parents' money for piano lessons, and that is where you feel most confident. Talk to the music director and let her know of your interest. What often happens with either new Christians or people who are new to a church is that they sit back and wait for someone to ask them to use their gifts. Then, when no one does, they become a bit put out about it.

How much better to let people know of your skills and then see where you can be used. By starting with an area of confidence, you decrease the risk of failing in this new venture called serving God.

Don't get in over your head

The great thing about new Christians is that they are usually the most excited about their faith. Having so recently experienced the tremendous contrast between the reality of salvation and the hopelessness of being lost, many Christians start off like gangbusters, getting involved in everything and witnessing to everybody. That enthusiasm should not be tampered with, but it must be tempered with the desire not to flame out in a short time. Try taking on one project or one area of service—keeping plenty of time for family and friends.

Expect to be lost at first

Remember that first day in a new job? When you decide to serve God by helping in the church or some other Christian organization, you can expect to feel a little out of place in the beginning. That's why it might be beneficial to sign up as a helper for some ministry for a while.

For instance, if you have an interest in witnessing, the best policy at first may be to go along with a more mature believer as you share your faith. Or if you want to teach preschoolers, sit in on a few sessions before taking on a class by yourself.

A rewarding experience

As you begin to contemplate what you can do in the church, it may encourage you to read a roll call of workers in the early church who received commendation by Paul for their efforts (see Romans 16). These were ordinary people who served God in an extraordinary way—so much so that their efforts have been immortalized in Scripture.

- Priscilla and Aquila risked their lives for Paul and held house church in their home
- Mary worked hard for fellow believers
- Andronicus and Junias were imprisoned with Paul
- Urbanus was a fellow worker
- Tryphena and Tryphosa were hard workers
- Tertius wrote down the letter Paul was sending
- Gaius served with hospitality

You may never receive this kind of recognition from other people, but if you use your gift faithfully to build up others and bring praise to God, you will one day hear our Savior say, "Well done, good and faithful servant" (Matthew 25:21). And that's the best reward of all.

Getting into the Word

What do these verses tell you about the role you have in the church?

- Acts 6:3
- Romans 12:6–8
- 1 Corinthians 12:1–11
- Colossians 1:28–29
- 2 Timothy 2:1–6

Thinking it through

Consider the following questions as you reflect on what you have read in this chapter.

- What frightens you about the possibility of working in the church? Whom can you talk to about this?
- Some of the jobs we do for the Lord are done outside the church. What are some opportunities you see as available to you?
- What bothers you about the way you see some things done in the name of the Lord? What motives, methods, or attitudes seem wrong?

Getting practical

Try these suggestions for applying what you have read.

- List as many of jobs as you can that are being done right now in your church. Which ones seem like options to you?
- Spend some time making an inventory of your interests and skills, perhaps writing down what you discover. Then think about how those skills might be used to honor God and serve Him.
- If your church has a class in helping you find your spiritual gifts, take it. If it doesn't, perhaps a pastor can recommend a seminar or a book that might help.

Exploring the subject further

These books will help you explore and apply your gifts in service for Christ.

- *Improving Your Serve*, Charles R. Swindoll
- *Let the Church be the Church*, Ray Ortlund
- *Well-intentioned Dragons*, Ray Ortlund

10

An Often Bumpy Road

What do I do when the going gets rough?

A casual glance at our family station wagon would never have revealed its sinister intent. It looked for all the world like a nice, friendly vehicle for hauling six people around town. When we bought it, we thought it would be tons of fun to own and drive.

At first. Then the transmission wouldn't go into second gear anymore.

When the transmission went bad, I started to do some soul-searching. I thought maybe it was my fault. What have I done wrong? I wondered. Haven't I been a good enough father? A loving enough husband? Should I read my Bible more?

Then I took the car in to the shop to get it fixed. The service manager added to my guilt.

"How do we know how you drove the car?" he demanded when I suggested meekly that perhaps the car was the problem. Then, narrowing his eyes and glaring at me like a 1950's schoolmarm, he asked, "How do we know you didn't damage the transmission getting it out of a snowbank?"

I had done nothing of the kind. Yet somehow I felt responsible for those gears' not meshing anymore. Setting aside my mistreatment, I paid my hard-earned money and got the thing fixed.

Not many months later, the transmission again stopped going from first to second gear.

I began to think a lot about the word persecution. I had tried to be good. I had taken care of the kids and my wife. I had stayed out of snowbanks. But what good did it do? My transmission and I were back in the shop.

If it wasn't my fault, surely it was some evil force at work. Maybe, as with the Old Testament hero Job, this was a test of my trust in God. Even though I was living right, my transmission was being taken away from me.

My ongoing relationship with the service manager at the dealership was on the decline. Although he no longer accused me of winter-time shenanigans, he wasn't about to agree with me that this mechanical device had been poorly repaired, designed, or constructed.

So, after he had his people fix it again, we parted ways. Me wondering if I should curse transmissions and die, and him hoping never to see my gearbox again.

He wouldn't.

But not because the transmission held up. It didn't. Soon it wouldn't even bother to get into first gear anymore.

And now I didn't know what to think about life and what causes car problems. I had no answers. Just one big question: "Why me?"

This time I had someone else fix my car. He was a nice man who didn't question my driving habits or insinuate that I was the first person with this kind of car to ever have transmission trouble. He said what I wanted to hear all along: "We've had a lot of trouble with this transmission."

With his help I discovered that my "TR-1140 over-drive discombobulation-driven, automated, trans-verse-mounted, torque converter transaxle" (at least that's what I think he called it) was designed about as well as the lenses on the Hubble Space Telescope.

I was finally beginning to see the light. My transmission trouble had nothing to do with spiritu-al considerations. Nor was it a Jobian test of my de-votion to God. But it did go a long way toward answering one of life's toughest questions, "Why me?"

I came to the conclusion that my transmission kept breaking down because it was designed and built by fallible people who make mistakes. And in this imperfect world, things are destined to come apart. It's all part of life in a world that has been messed up by the original sin of Adam and the grief that sin has continued to cause.

All of the material things we depend on and think of as so important to our everyday well-being were built with the finite wisdom and from the finite perspective of human beings. They are temporary, decaying conveniences. They break down, become obsolete, cause frustration, and drain our resources. We cannot depend on them.

Yet we often consider the fate of so many of our modern conveniences as somehow being signs from God. We tend to think that the troubles we have be-cause the washer goes out are somehow the result of God's intervention in our life.

As we try to grapple with the struggles and trials we face—difficulties that many times make a faulty transmission seem inconsequential—it might help to put our troubles into two categories. In this way we can distinguish the difference between tough times that have a heavenly purpose and those that are just a part of existing on this less-than-perfect planet. Notice that in both situations, God is active—since He has total power in our lives and all that goes on in our world. In one He directs and in the other He allows. The shade of difference may seem small, but as we look at two biblical incidents—one from the Old Testament and one from the New, we can see that the distinction is vital.

Shooting ourselves in the foot

First, we sometimes have to deal with the God-directed, growth-producing trials that are part of life in a world ruled by God. This may be a novel concept to you if you are newly come to faith. It may sound highly unusual to hear someone talk about a higher purpose behind the problems we face. Generally speaking, people in our society view all of their problems somewhat fatalistically. They say that things simply happen for no apparent reason and with no real cause. The only thing we can do when struggles and tragedies visit us, they say, is to grin and bear it. "Nothing happens on purpose," is their credo.

Perhaps you have heard the story of Jonah, an Old Testament prophet. His story is told in the book of the Bible that bears his name. Briefly, here's what happened to him: God commanded Jonah to go to the city of Ninevah to preach against the wickedness that was so prevalent there. Jonah, however, decided to run away to a place called Tarshish, so he boarded a boat that would take him there. As the boat made its way across the water, a huge storm arose. The seamen cast lots (similar to drawing straws) to see who had done something to cause this trouble, and the lot fell on Jonah.

After some debate, the men tossed Jonah into the water, where he was swallowed by a huge fish that God had prepared especially for Jonah. That fish was Jonah's home for the next three days as he learned his lesson about the foolishness of disobeying God.

Jonah did not know what problems can result when things go wrong inside a transmission, but he sure found out what can go wrong inside a huge fish. Jonah's predicament was his own fault. He knew exactly what God wanted him to do, but he did the opposite. As he contemplated his future from the smelly belly of a God-prepared fish, he knew he had put himself there. He was disobedient to God's clear demands, and he paid for it.

Often we get swallowed up in huge problems that are a direct result of our disobedience. We allow anger to make us sin by hurting others, and we end up struggling to restore those relationships. We covet what we cannot afford and allow ourselves to get into debt. One makes up a story to cover an error, only to discover that one has dug a hole too deep to get out of. A little disobedience can get us into big trouble.

The good news is that Jonah did not stay in the belly of the fish. He called out to God and recommitted himself to doing what he knew all along was right. God heard his confession and the fish delivered Jonah onto the beach as only a fish can.

Although nothing could erase from Jonah's mind the memory of that disgusting ride in the Mediterranean, he was given a second chance to do what God commanded. That is the hope for all of us who face trials that we bring on ourselves with our errors.

We can ask God's forgiveness and begin again to do the things God has, in His Word, instructed us to do. We begin to solve the problem with confession, then comes God's forgiveness, then comes our obedience. When we follow that pattern, trials can be transformed into triumphs—even when the trials are of our own making.

Raining on the just and the unjust

The second kind of trouble that comes to us in this world is the God-allowed problem that results from the state of the world in which we live. Remember, just because you are now a Christian, you have no promise of trouble-free living on this side of heaven. Some of the difficulties you will face, just like my struggles with that broken-down, old transmission, are simply a part of life in a world that has been cursed by sin.

Once when Jesus was talking to a large crowd, some of his listeners told of an incident during which Pilate had ordered some Galileans killed while they were making sacrifices. Jesus explained to the gathering that those people should not be considered worse sinners because they died that way. Then He mentioned another incident in which seemingly innocent people met their deaths.

"Those eighteen who died when the tower in Siloam fell on them—do you think they were more guilty than all the others living in Jerusalem?" Jesus asked them. "I tell you, no!" (Luke 13:4–5) In these two tragedies, bad things happened to what were probably good people. And this led the crowd to wonder. Perhaps they thought that those who died were guilty of some secret sins for which they were being punished. Jesus assured them that was not the case.

But then how do we rationalize such tragedies? Why does death strike innocent people in our world—through murder and cruelty, through natural disasters, or even through disease that visits us through no fault of our own? Some would look at these random incidences and say that either God is not there or He doesn't care.

That response, however, misses the point. The point is that, except for the cleansing power of Jesus Christ, we are all guilty before God. In that sense, there are no "innocent victims." Those of us who are fortunate enough in God's sovereignty to make it through another day unscathed ought to be praising and thanking Him. Rather than wondering why suffering hits some people and not others, we ought to be marveling that any of us are left at all.

Good out of evil

Whatever we think about bad things and why they occur, we have to consider carefully these words of the Lord: "I am the Lord, and there is no other. I form the light and create darkness, I bring prosperity and create disaster; I, the Lord do all these things" (Isaiah45:6–7). When God moves on the earth, either in what we consider happy circumstances or in what we consider trials and difficulties, we know that He moves with a purpose.

Imagine standing at Golgotha on the day of Jesus' crucifixion. Imagine being one of the disciples, those eleven friends of His who had seen Jesus handle every situation with perfection. Imagine wondering what God was doing to this gentle carpenter's son who was suffering the most painful, inhumane death the Romans could devise. Imagine hearing Him groan and finally give up with the words, "My God! My God! Why have You forsaken Me?"

Don't you think those friends of Jesus wondered how God could have allowed such a despicable thing to happen to Him? What was the point, they must have asked each other.

Their questions began to be answered just three days later when they saw the resurrected Christ. As the weeks went by, they began to see that God caused suffering of this Innocent One for a purpose that went far beyond anything they could imagine.

We need that perspective. We need to see that God's purposes in the trials and tragedies of our lives may not be clear to us right away. Actually, we may never fully understand. But our ignorance of God's purposes need not cause us to question His goodness, greatness, graciousness, and mercy.

Through the comfort, empowerment, and strength of the Holy Spirit, we can love and trust God enough to accept what He sends our way— whether it's nothing more than a faulty transmission or a nothing less than a fearful tragedy.

Guidelines for handling adversity

The more you grow to know and love God, the more astounded you will be with the many ways His Word helps us make it through this life. Because God was

aware that we all suffer problems of various sorts
and because He cares so deeply for us, He has told
us what we can do to lessen the hurt when problems
come into our lives.

Turn over your troubles to God

"Cast all your anxiety on him because he cares for
you" (1 Peter 5:7).

Children know exactly where to go when trouble
hits. A skinned knee, a scary bully, or a lost pet all
send children running to Mom or Dad. Kids know
where to go to find someone who will fix scrapes, run
off bullies, and find pets.

Christians have a Father to whom we can go. We
can be sure of His open arms to gather us in, His listening ears to hear us, and His promises of help to
sustain us. Most of all, we have the knowledge that
"He cares" (1 Peter 5:7). The caring of a loving, kind,
and compassionate parent is what gets children past
their troubles; the caring of a heavenly Father can
help us work through ours. We need only to bow in
prayer and unburden our hearts, open our Bibles
and discover His promises, and rest in His loving
care.

Do not worry

"Therefore I tell you, do not worry about your life,
what you will eat or drink; or about your body, what
you will wear" (Matthew 6:25).

Telling a worrier not to worry is almost like telling a dog not to bark. Worrying, though, has less value than a good healthy bark, and it can be avoided.

Worrying doesn't do any good. "Who of you by
worrying can add a single hour to his life?" (Matthew

6:27). Worry never stopped a problem from happening; it never kept a child safe; it never made the weather change; it never made anything happen. All worry does is make us miserable about things that probably won't happen anyway.

What counts when problems are on the horizon are two things: action, and trust in God. If we can take action to avoid the problem, we should do it—but worrying is not such an action. If we feel that there is nothing we can do, we can take comfort in knowing that God is never in that predicament. He can always act on our behalf, which means we can always seek God's care and ask His Spirit for guidance and strength.

Take comfort from God

"Praise be to the God and Father of our Lord Jesus Christ, the Father of compassion and the God of all comfort, who comforts us in all our troubles, so that we can comfort those in any trouble with the comfort we ourselves have received from God" (2 Corinthians 1:3–4).

It's going to happen. Trouble is going to hit. What can enable us live without fear is the fact that, when we run into difficulty, we know where to turn. Christian, you are promised twice the comfort anyone else will receive. First, you have a loving, gentle, compassionate, righteous, perfect Father to wrap His arms of care around you and soothe your hurt. God is One who knows of the need for comfort, for He Himself suffered when Jesus hung on the cross enduring the pain of all humankind's sin. And as the One who made our emotions, no one knows better than He how to calm them. Our first place to turn, then, when life smacks us in the face is to our "God of all comfort."

The second part of this dual comfort treatment comes from our fellow believers. Those who have faced their own trials, which is just about everyone, have had the opportunity to learn from God about comfort and therefore can transfer that knowledge to those who hurt. Here's the formula: God comforts the believer and the believer comforts a fellow believer. When we let it work, our troubles seem less burdensome because we share the load.

Take life a day at a time

"Therefore do not worry about tomorrow, for tomorrow will worry about itself. Each day has enough trouble of its own" (Matthew 6:34)

Life is hard enough with just the struggles we have to face today. There is no wisdom in taking on tomorrow's problems and adding them to what may be an already full plate today.

Tomorrow can loom large on the horizon, casting backward shadows across the landscape of today—if we let it. We can prepare to face tomorrow and do all we can to avoid difficulties that might come, but we have no way of knowing today if tomorrow will bring harm or good. That's why it is so important that we take seriously Jesus' words about worrying. As my son Stevie said, during his kindergarten year, when I was trying to explain the concepts of today and tomorrow, "It's never tomorrow."

When you face the end of this day and look back on it, you can see how, in spite of the problems that came along, God gave you the grace to make it through. He promised us, as He promised the apos-

tle Paul, "My grace is sufficient for you" (2 Corinthians 12:9). Yet we often want more than that. We
want grace for the difficulties of tomorrow today. His
grace is new every morning (Lamentations 3:23). We
can't get a two-day supply.

The problem of problems will be with us as long as
we are on this earth. The sin of humankind has
guaranteed that. Although it is in God's plan to
eventually eliminate all of the struggles we experience, He allows us now to live in a world where tragedies, accidents, heartache, and evil seem to be
everywhere. Doubters may wonder at this plan—
questioning how a good God can allow these difficulties. But if we will have complete faith in the God
who is too infinitely wise to make a mistake, too perfect to falter, and too loving to let us struggle without
His loving care, we can demonstrate the way God
works on earth. We can show that in a sin-darkened
and damaged world, God's light illumines the path-
way to true happiness. We can display the power of
God to care for His own and to transform ordinary
people into ambassadors of the great message of salvation.

On this side of heaven, we will face problems. It
is our godly reaction to them and our dependence on
God through them that conquers our difficulties and
turns tragedies into triumphs.

Getting into the Word
What promises of God's help in the time of difficulty
can you find in these passages?
  • Psalm 23
  • Psalm 27:10

- Psalm 41:3
- Psalm 42:5
- Psalm 51:17
- Psalm 55:22
- Romans 8:18
- Romans 8:35–39
- 2 Corinthians 5:1
- 2 Thessalonians 2:16–17
- James 5:11
- 1 Peter 2:21

Thinking it through

Consider the following questions as you reflect on what you have read in this chapter.

- What problems have been most on your mind recently? Have you thought of the possibility of turning them over to God instead of worrying about them yourself?
- As you look at the question of problems from your new perspective as a Christian, what still bothers you about the fact that you have problems?
- When you hear someone preaching or teaching that you don't have to have problems if you have enough faith, what should your reaction be?
- What problems did the faithful people in the Bible (for example, Moses, Joseph, Job, David, Peter, Paul) have even though they had great faith? How did they handle them?
- Have your problems increased or decreased since you became a believer in Jesus? What lessons can you learn from that?

Getting practical

Try these suggestions for applying what you have read.

> • List all the things that might go wrong tomorrow. Tomorrow evening, go over the list and see how things turned out.
>
> • Learn some praise songs or choruses by listening to tapes or to a Christian radio station. When troubles hit, sing a praise song, pray, and give the problem to God.
>
> • Make a chart of the difficulties you have encountered in the past week. Put them under two headings: Personal errors and Unavoidable problems. Consider those problems that result from mistakes as lessons learned. Turn the unavoidable problems into prayer requests.

Exploring the subject further

If you'd like to read more about problems in the life of the Christian and how to handle them, look at these books.

> • *Where Is God When It Hurts?* Philip Yancey
> • *Broken Things,* M.R. De Haan
> • *Why Am I Crying?* Martha Maughon
> • *Bruised But Not Broken: Finding Strength for Your Hard Times,* Stanley C. Baldwin
> • *The Problem of Pain,* C. S. Lewis

11

A New Way of Relating

How do I get along with people?

A woman employed by a Christian ministry was talking one morning with an electrician who had come to try to finish up some work he was doing on an addition to the building. The added space was quite large, and the workers had been on the job for a long time. This particular day, however, was supposed to be their last.

The electrician explained to the woman that if they could not get the job done that day, their contract called for a fine of several hundred dollars to be levied against the electrical company for each extra day they had to work.

The woman did not know if the man was a believer in Jesus Christ or not, so she measured her words carefully. Thinking of the testimony of the organization, she left the man with this comment: "If you don't make your deadline, you just remind our people that this is a Christian organization."

Without being too forward, she was trying to convey that when you deal with Christians, you are dealing with people who are different from the norm—people who are forgiving and understanding.

Of course, it would have been perfectly legal and eth-
ical for the ministry to dock the electrical company
for not hitting the target deadline, but the woman
was hoping a more godly principle might override
their concern for money.

Christians, this woman had been taught, operate under some different guidelines for getting along
with people—principles that should make us the
kind of people others want to be around, get to
know, befriend, and do business with. Getting along
with others takes on an entirely new dimension
when a person has a personal relationship with
Christ.

Forgive as you have been forgiven

"Bear with each other and forgive whatever grievanc-
es you may have against one another. Forgive as the
Lord forgave you" (Colossians 3:13).

A story Jesus told sets the tone for the attitude
we need to demonstrate when someone does something to us that we do not find acceptable. It contrasts greatly with the accepted reaction in our day,
which is advertised so proudly on bumper stickers
that say, "I don't get mad, I get even." That way of
thinking is at odds with how a Christian, who has
been forgiven so much, should respond.

Here's how Jesus explained the attitude of forgiveness to Peter, who wanted to know how many
times a person should be forgiven. In Matthew
18:21–35, the Savior told about a king who was busy
settling accounts with his servants. One of the servants brought before him was obviously not a money
wizard. He owed the king ten thousand talents,
which today would be equivalent to millions of dol-

lars. In that society, the only answer was that the servant, his family, and his possessions be sold to pay the debt. This understandably worried the servant, so he fell down at the king's feet and begged his master to have patience with him.

Moved by this request, the king forgave the man's debt and let him go. This action set the example of forgiveness, but somehow the forgiven servant didn't get the point. He promptly went out and nabbed a fellow servant who owed him a hundred denarii—which was far less than one percent of what he had owed the king. The fellow servant couldn't pay, so the one who had been forgiven by the king had him thrown into jail until he could pay off the lousy hundred denarii.

As you might imagine, when word got back to the king about this he was livid. He had the unforgiving servant picked up and hauled off to some nasty people who tortured him until he paid off the debt.

This story makes the matter of forgiveness about as clear as it can be. We are the forgiven servant. Jesus has forgiven us our debt—one that we could never repay in a million years. Instead of languishing in the debtors prison of hell for an eternity—which is where we deserve to go—we will be in God's presence forever. We have been forgiven even more than that servant. Our test is how we turn around and treat others. Are we, who were forgiven so much, as forgiving with those who owe us? Or do we, like this ungrateful servant, always demand what is coming to us? We need to remember Jesus' haunting words as He concluded His parable: "This is how my heavenly Father will treat each of you unless you forgive your brother from your heart" (Matthew 18:35).

Love others

"Love your neighbor as yourself" (Romans 13:9).

If we can get a handle on this simple five-word sentence, our efforts to get along with others will be successful. When Paul wrote these words to the people at the church of Rome, he provided them with three accompanying truths that clearly defined how to love someone so completely.

First, he said, "Let no debt remain outstanding, except the continuing debt to love one another" (Romans 13:8). Think of the contrast between the two kinds of debts represented here. When we owe our neighbor something like a borrowed wheelbarrow, we always run the risk of negative feelings. We might say, "I wonder if he thinks I'm taking too many loads of dirt with this thing." And he might worry aloud, "He had better take care of that borrowed barrow!" But if we owe nothing but love, everything is positive. When I know that my neighbor will give me nothing but love and understanding, our relationship will always be strong and honest.

Second, Paul made an astounding statement about this idea of loving our neighbors as we do ourselves. He said that all the other commandments are summed up in this single statement (13:9). In other words, when we love our neighbors, friends, coworkers, and others as we do ourselves, we won't be trapped by the sins of murder, stealing, lying, coveting, or committing adultery. The right kind of love, then, is a safeguard against any kind of sin in which we misuse others.

Paul's third statement is much like that one. He said, "Love does no harm to its neighbor" (13:10). Christian love manifested toward those with whom we come in contact has the same characteristics of Jesus' love for those with whom He walked this earth: it refuses to hurt others.

Avoid foolish arguments

"Avoid foolish controversies and genealogies and arguments and quarrels about the law, because these are unprofitable and useless" (Titus 3:9).

One thing that you will discover in your dealings with other believers is that Christians hold a wide variety of opinions on what the Bible says about certain subjects. You will find people disagreeing about such matters as the right way to baptize, whether or not to speak in tongues, whether a church should have deacons or elders, what kind of music to listen to in the church, whether Christians will be taken away by Christ in the air, what kind of church services are the most biblical, and many, many other topics.

On many of these matters we will never agree until we see our Savior in heaven. Only then will the final authority on these matters speak. Until then, the arguments will go on.

Scholars on both sides of issues will continue to research and write papers detailing their positions. And the people in the churches will continue to wonder who is right.

Paul seems to be saying that is often best to avoid the trouble that is brewed during arguments. Some issues are worth standing up for, such as who God is, the inerrancy of the Bible, the person and work of Christ, salvation through faith, the hope of heaven and the fear of hell, the importance of the church, the need for daily growth in the Word and prayer, the importance of evangelism, and the hope of Jesus' return. Protect these doctrines, for they are not foolish disputes. But in dealing with people with whom you disagree, still remember that you should love them as yourself and you should talk to them with patience and humility.

Keep the record clean

"If you are offering your gift at the altar and there remember that your brother has something against you, leave your gift there in front of the altar. First go and be reconciled to your brother; then come and offer your gift" (Matthew 5:23–24).

Reconciliation first, then worship. That, in essence, is the pattern we need to develop. We might think that because worshiping God is so important it should always be our top priority. But according to the words of Jesus, God does not want our worship until we first make sure we are reconciled to any person with whom we have been having a problem.

In this teaching, we are not told who has committed the error that caused the need for reconciliation. It seems not to matter who is at fault; the problem needs to be rectified by the one who is getting ready to enter the presence of the Lord in praise, prayer, and adoration.

Reconciliation first, then worship. It's a guideline worth remembering.

Matthew 18 gives us some specific guidelines on accomplishing that reconciliation when someone "sins against" us. Remembering that forgiveness is always the order of the day for believers in Jesus, we will want to look for a solution that restores the relationship, not one that makes matters worse. Here is how Jesus said to do that.

First, "go and show him his fault, just between the two of you" (Matthew 18:15). In private, you or I should get together with the one who has offended and explain what the offense is. Again, we need to keep in mind that humility, patience, and love are always traits we carry with us into any such confrontations. If it works, Jesus said, "you have won your brother over" (18:15). The record is clean and your relationship is restored.

Sometimes, as you may have guessed, things don't go according to Plan A. In that case, Jesus provided Plan B.

"But if he will not listen, take one or two others along" (18:16). This is not to team up against the offender, but to help that person see the seriousness of the offense.

Not surprisingly, this may fail also, given the nature of people. "If he refuses to listen to them," Jesus says, drastic measures are required. "Tell it to the church; and if he refuses even to hear the church, treat him as you would a pagan" (18:17).

At this point, you have done all you can. Still holding out the promise of forgiveness if the offender wants it, you can go on in life with a clean conscience, knowing that the next step must be the offender's.

Make your love practical

"Suppose a brother or sister is without clothes and daily food. If one of you says to him, 'Go, I wish you well; keep warm and well fed,' but does nothing about his physical needs, what good is it?" (James 2:14–15)

It doesn't do anyone any good if we are the most loving Christians in the world if we spend all of our time in the den watching old John Wayne movies. We have to get out of the house and practice our love on others. Love that is not exercised is not very valuable. Think of how God demonstrated His love toward us: He left heaven, came to earth in the person of Jesus, lived a lowly existence, and died on the cross to ensure our eternal life. Had God stayed in heaven and felt love for us yet never acted, how would we know of His love?

A love that does not show up in our actions toward others is hypocrisy. The apostle Paul, in Romans 12, tells us how to avoid that kind of hypocrisy. He tells us how to put some feet on our love.

- Be kindly affectionate to one another (12:10).
- Honor one another above yourselves (12:10).
- Share with God's people who are in need (12:13).
- Practice hospitality (12:13).
- Bless those who persecute you (12:14).
- Rejoice with those who rejoice; mourn with those who mourn (12:15).
- Live peaceably with everyone, as much as you can (12:18).
- Take care of your enemy (12:20).

Each of these actions will help us make our love practical. Many of these activities are characteristic of the best charitable organizations in our society. We should be challenged to make sure we Christians are noted for our works of love, because the testimony of our faith often depends on it. With love in action as our goal, we can find dozens of ways to make a practical difference in the lives of those who need our help.

Control your tongue

"Let your conversation always be full of grace, seasoned with salt, so that you may know how to answer everyone" (Colossians 4:6).

In our relationships with others, one part of the body gets us in more trouble than any other—the tongue. If what we say is not gracious and sensible, we will find ourselves putting out little fires of contention that the tongue (which James 3:6 calls "a fire") ignites.

Perhaps before you were saved you often found yourself saying things you later regretted. Even if you have been a Christian for a while you may realize that your words are sometimes not pleasing to God. The Bible tells us many things about the tongue, and gives us some principles and helpful advice that might help you keep your tongue in check.

Don't whine

"Do everything without complaining or arguing" (Philippians 2:14).

Isn't it ironic that in our land of plenty we have become a nation of gripers? In homes where the VCR is plugged in, both cars are snugly parked in the garage, and the refrigerator holds enough food to feed a hundred starving Somalians, we still find things about which to complain.

Paul suggests a better attitude. Rather than facing each task with a spirit of dissatisfaction, one should hold off on the grumbling. In fact, to take it a step further, we might consider the truth that when we go ahead and perform tasks we didn't want to do, we can turn negatives into positives. For instance, we have all experienced the frustration of sitting down to a relaxing evening with a good book and having someone interrupt the quiet with a call for help. Perhaps it is a child who needs help with homework, a neighbor whose car won't start, or a friend who needs a listening ear.

In those situations, we could grumble, complain, and say no, which would make two people upset. Or we can provide the service needed. If we do, we discover that not only does the person who made the request benefit, but so do we. An attitude of service beats an attitude of grumbling anytime.

When we put that principle into practice, we make progress toward becoming the kind of Christians who draw people to Christ.

Resist hurtful speaking

"Rid yourselves of all malice and all deceit, hypocrisy, envy, and slander of every kind" (1 Peter 2:1).

Words can be bad or they can be good. Bad words can come from our lips. Good words, actually the best words, come from the Word of God. Peter contrasts those two choices in 1 Peter 2:1–2. Our hurtful speaking, which we need to get rid of, contrasts greatly with "the pure milk of the Word," which we need to desire. If we desire the latter, we will find less and less use for the former.

Listen more than you speak

"Everyone should be quick to listen, slow to speak and slow to become angry" (James 1:19).

The story is told of a smug, sophisticated Englishman driving his roadster proudly down a country road. As he neared a sharp, blind curve, he noticed an oncoming car careening around the bend with dust flying and tires skidding. The driver, a woman, successfully regained control of her car just before it came parallel to the gentleman's car. She slowed down just long enough to yell, "Pig!" at the man. Then she sped off.

Startled by all this, the man reacted quickly. He knew he had not been hogging the road, so he aimed his tongue at her and fired off a loud, "Horse!" her way as she rushed off.

Proud of his ability to respond so quickly with a verbal blast of his own, the man put the pedal to the metal and took off around the bend . . . and ran right into the pig the woman had been trying to warn him about.

It is natural for us to respond as quickly as we can to supposed hurts—to assume that the other person has it in for us so we had better let that person have it. But we don't have to. We can respond supernaturally once we have Jesus as our Savior and the Holy Spirit living within us. The Christian way to respond to people is spelled out for us in James 1:19, where the writer suggests this approach:

Listen swiftly.

Speak slowly.

Grow angry slowly.

We learn more when we listen than we do when we talk. We get in trouble more when we talk than we do when we listen. And we stop listening and start talking too much when we grow angry. How much it will help our relationships with others—and our testimony for Jesus Christ—if we listen better, talk less, and avoid anger!

Choose your close relationships among Christians

"Do not be yoked together with unbelievers" (2 Corinthians 6:14).

If you are a new Christian just getting accustomed to the teachings of the Bible, this one may seem at first to be a huge contradiction. Throughout this chapter, we have been talking about how you can get along with others; how love is of utmost importance; how you should help people and talk to them the right way and befriend them.

Then here comes this verse. It seems to be so exclusive in an age where inclusiveness is the accepted norm. After all, aren't we supposed to accept and love everyone? Isn't it "Christian" not to be prejudiced or reject people because of their beliefs?

The principle behind the teaching is simple. In 1 Corinthians 6:14–16, Paul poses a series of rhetorical questions. He asks how righteousness and lawlessness can coexist. Or light and darkness. Or Christ and the devil. Or a believer and an unbeliever. The matter of faith in Jesus Christ is a serious subject—one that makes the believer a special person who has given self over completely to God. How can one who accepts Jesus by faith associate intimately with someone who scoffs at that faith?

Faith in Christ is not something that rests alone in a small section of a person's heart and life. It permeates all of life; it becomes the essence of who you are. It is not like signing up to play for the Detroit Tigers this year, knowing that next year you might sign a contract with the Toronto Blue Jays. Being a Christian is permanent and serious.

It means being adopted into a family of which the non-Christian is not a member. It means living by a set of guidelines that are perfect and right, yet very different from the standards of the world It means having a totally different outlook on life.

As hard as it might be to understand, it is good and right that we make our fast, intimate relationships with those who share our faith. It is wrong for us to be hooked together with those who oppose our membership in God's family through Jesus. And it is appropriate that we respond with the right actions when we see how important this principle is in the life of faith.

Those actions first include doing all we can to win our loved ones, friends, and associates to Jesus Christ. What better way to share our love with them than to share the best news that we have ever heard!

Share your faith

"Go into all the world and preach the good news" (Mark 16:15)

Part of getting along with those who stand on the other side of the Cross from us includes doing all we can to help them see the advantages, the urgency, and the absolute necessity of accepting Jesus Christ as their Savior. In the remainder of this chapter, then, we will look at some biblical, practical ways to let those people with whom we share our lives but not our faith know how they, too, can be rescued.

Be ready to explain

"Always be prepared to give an answer to everyone

who asks you to give the reason for the hope that you have" (1 Peter 3:15).

Christianity is a very reasonable faith. If you look around at other religions, you will see that many demands made on their adherents are both ridiculous and fruitless. One Eastern religion requires ritual washings in a grotesquely polluted river while asking that devotees treat beasts of burden as holy. Others demand injurious pilgrimages or backbreaking stair climbs. Some ask people to depend on dead prophets or highly questionable documents. Still others depend on long-dead people communicating with one supposed "channeler," who usually makes tons of money with those exclusive rights.

Christianity is different. You can study its book and depend on its accuracy. You can see the difference it makes in the lives of so many. You can worship the one true God and know in your heart that He is there. You can trust the historicity, the clarity, the believability, and the reality of the Christian faith. It alone can stand up to attack and defeat attack with evidence that is provable.

Your job, then, is to become familiar enough with the Bible and its teachings that you can readily "give the reason for the hope that you have" (1 Peter 2:15).

Say it with actions

"Let your light shine before men, that they may see your good deeds and praise your Father in heaven" (Matthew 5:16).

Jesse Barfield is a baseball player who once hit forty home runs for the Toronto Blue Jays. But his favorite story is not about his ability to hit the long ball. He enjoys telling about Roy Lee Jackson, a relief pitcher and Barfield's teammate when he first joined the Jays. Barfield likes to tell about the time he first saw Jackson in action in the locker room after he lost a ballgame. Barfield expected Jackson to blow up and throw things around. Instead he calmly got dressed and went home. Later, when Jackson won a game, Barfield expected some act of pride or egotism. Instead, Jackson again calmly got dressed and went home.

Those two incidents led Barfield to investigate what was different about Roy Lee Jackson. And they gave Jackson the opportunity to lead Jesse Barfield to faith in Christ. Jackson let his light shine so brightly that his teammate could not help but see it.

When Jesus said, "Let your light shine," He made no mention of a lot of words. No mention of handing out tracts or knocking on doors. Just a reference to a lifestyle that shows people the difference in your life. For Roy Lee Jackson, letting his light shine meant his quiet acceptance of whatever came his way. For you it might mean doing your job at work without complaining. It might mean being a loving, kind, generous, understanding spouse to an unsaved mate. It might mean helping a young mother with her children. It might mean shopping for an elderly neighbor.

President George Bush didn't start anything new with his thousand points of light. For two thousand years, believers of Jesus have been points of light, using their commitment to Jesus as shining beacons to light the path to God for the unsaved.

It worked for Roy Lee Jackson when his shining light influenced Jesse Barfield to ask about his faith.

Then Jackson could "give the reason for the hope" that he has.

Give no offense

"Do not cause anyone to stumble" (1 Corinthians 10:32).

It sometimes seems that the religious people who have been in the media spotlight the most in the past few years have neglected this teaching. We have seen courtroom trials of people professing to be Christian leaders. We've seen others exposed on news programs as charlatans. We've heard of pastor after pastor who has succumbed to some sin that has scandalized the community. On a very large scale, we have seen how fellow believers can give so much offense that unbelievers just laugh when we try to present Christianity to them.

One of our main tasks is to live so that the glory for our lives goes to God and so that no one is left questioning faith in Jesus Christ. A life of no offense is one of the greatest testimonies for the Savior, and Paul tells us how to accomplish it.

First he writes, "Nobody should seek his own good, but the good of others" (1 Corinthians 10:24). To show Christlikeness, we must have this attitude, which was displayed by Jesus Himself. He spent a lifetime looking out for others and not thinking of Himself.

Next Paul gives us an example of a situation in which one is asked not to do something that in one's mind is acceptable. Instead of arguing and making sure one's rights are honored, Paul suggests that the person agree to avoid the offending behavior. This is part of doing everything "to the glory of God" (10:31), which contrasts so strongly with what we would do otherwise—doing things to our own glory. It is all part of giving no offense, which Paul says, will result in "the good of many, so that they may be saved" (10:33).

Start close to home

"You will be my witnesses in Jerusalem, and in all Judea and Samaria, and to the ends of the earth" (Acts 1:8).

The call to help others know Christ is more than something we do because we want to avoid the inconvenient alliances about which 1 Corinthians 6:14 talks. It is a command of Jesus Himself. He said that we have a responsibility to tell the entire world of His story (Matthew 28:19), and He laid out a plan for doing so. We are to be witnesses of Jesus' gospel first where we live (Jerusalem); then in the surrounding areas (Judea and Samaria); and then spread the word to the ends of the earth. There is no other calling as important as this one.

Getting into the Word

The New Testament frequently uses the phrase *one another* or *each other* as we are instructed in how to live as lights in the world. What do these "one another" verses tell us about getting along with people—both fellow believers and those who do not know Jesus?

- John 13:34–35
- John 15:12
- Acts 7:26
- Romans 12:5
- Romans 12:10

- Romans 13:8
- Romans 14:13
- Romans 15:7
- Romans 15:14
- 1 Corinthians 6:7
- Galatians 5:13–15
- Ephesians 4:2
- Ephesians 4:32
- Ephesians 5:21
- Colossians 3:9
- Colossians 3:13
- Colossians 3:16
- 1 Thessalonians 4:18
- 1 Thessalonians 5:11

Thinking it through

Consider the following questions as you reflect on what you have read in this chapter.

- Which of these words best describe you and your relationship with others?

❏ Kind
❏ Compassionate
❏ Loving
❏ Arrogant
❏ Easily angered
❏ Pushy
❏ Grouchy
❏ Understanding

What can you do to make sure the right words are used when your name comes up?

- If someone were to meet you for the first time today and then observe you for a week, what traits or actions would lead them to think that you have a special relationship with God?

• What keeps you from telling others about your faith? Are these good reasons or bad excuses?

• Why is it so important to live in such a way that others will be impressed favorably? Why is it so much more important for Christians than it is for non-Christians?

Getting practical

Try these suggestions for applying what you have read.

• Write down the names of five people you would like to introduce to Jesus in the next year. Next to each name, write one way (perhaps from those given in this chapter) you can start.

• List the "problem people" in your life right now. What steps can you take to turn them into friends? What could God be teaching you by having you work with or be related to or go to church with these problem people?

• Look at the "one another" passages listed above. Which ones are naturally easy to accomplish and which are a real chore?

Exploring the subject further

The following books are excellent resources for more guidance on sharing your faith.

• *How to Give Away Your Faith*, Paul E. Little

• *Life-Style Evangelism*, Joseph Aldridge

• *How Can I Share My Faith Without an Argument?*, Bill Faye (available free through Radio Bible Class)

• *Living Proof*, Jim Peterson

Appendix A

Words Worth Knowing

If you are new in the Christian faith, you often hear terms, phrases, and words that are not a part of your working vocabulary. To help you become literate as a student of the Bible, here is a list of words you need to know as you begin to communicate your faith and communicate with people of faith.

Aaron: the brother of Moses. (See Exodus 4:14.)

Abba, Father: A name we can use to call out to God, indicating His fatherly relationship to us. It is somewhat akin to saying, "Daddy." (See Romans 8:15.)

Abraham: The founder of the Jewish nation. He was an ancestor of Christ. (See Genesis 11 and following.)

Abrahamic covenant: A promise God made to Abraham that he and his descendants, the people of Israel, would have special favor with God. (See Genesis 12.)

Adam and Eve: Our original parents, created by a separate special act of God. (See Genesis 2.)

agnostic: A person who is not sure whether God exists or not.

Alpha and Omega: Names used to describe God, meaning He is the beginning and the end. (See Revelation 22:13.)

Andrew: One of the disciples. (See Matthew 4:18.)

angels: Ministering spirits who have been sent forth to aid believing people. (See Hebrews 1:14.)

Antichrist: A person who will one day set up a government on earth and try to overthrow Jesus in a battle at the end of time as we know it. (See 1 John 2:18, 22.)

Antioch: A town in Syria where the believers were first given the name Christian. (See Acts 11:19–26.)

apologetics: The study of how we defend the faith.

apostles: First-century followers of Jesus and the leaders of the Christian faith. The first twelve apostles were Simon Peter, Andrew, James, John, Philip, Bartholomew, Thomas, Matthew, James, Thaddaeus, Simon the Canaanite, and Judas Iscariot. (See Matthew 10:3–4.)

ark: The boat God told Noah to build so he and his family could escape the great flood that was sent on the earth as a judgment. (See Genesis 6–8.)

ark of the covenant: A container built for the tabernacle when the children of Israel were wandering in the desert for forty years. The ark was kept in the Holy of Holies (the most holy place) and contained Aaron's rod that budded, along with some manna and the Ten Commandments. (See Exodus 37:1–9.)

Armageddon: In biblical prophesy, this is the last great battle on earth before Jesus sets up His kingdom. (See Revelation 16:16.)

atheism: The belief that there is no God. (See Psalm 14:1.)

Augustus Caesar: Ruler of Rome. He was emperor when Jesus was born. (See Luke 2:1.)

Babel: Here the descendents of Noah built a tall tower, thinking they could reach God and make a name for themselves. It was at this time that God created various languages and thus confounded their efforts. (See Genesis 11:1–9.)

Babylon: A country that was Israel's enemy. God allowed Babylon to take over Israel and keep the people captive as a result of their disobedience to Him. (See 2 Kings 17.)

baptism: The act of immersing or sprinkling a person with the water as a sign and seal of God's claim on his or her life. (See Acts 8:26–38.)

Barabbas: A murderer who was let go so Jesus would be crucified. (See Matthew 27:15–26.)

Bathsheba: A woman with whom King David committed adultery, thus beginning a string of sad events. (See 2 Samuel 11–12.)

Beatitudes: A part of Jesus' Sermon on the Mount, it gives us guidelines for how we should live. (See Matthew 5:3–12.)

Bethlehem: The town where Jesus was born. (See Luke 2:1–12.)

body of Christ: A term that is often used to describe the people in the church; in other words, people who are believers in Jesus Christ. (See 1 Corinthians 12:27.)

born again: A term used often to describe the process of becoming a Christian. (See John 3.)

burning bush: God appeared to Moses in a bush that burned but was not consumed. (See Exodus 3:3.)

Calvary: The place where Jesus was crucified. Also referred to as Golgotha.

Canaan: The promised land that the people of Israel finally occupied after forty years of wilderness wanderings. (See Exodus 6:4.)

coat of many colors: A robe that Jacob gave to his son

Joseph. It made Joseph's brothers jealous enough to want to kill him. (See Genesis 37.)

communion: The celebration of the Lord's Supper, commemorating the death of Jesus. (See 1 Corinthians 11:17–34.)

Creation: The act of God by which our world and everything in it was created out of nothing. (See Genesis 1 and Colossians 1:16.)

cross: The wooden implement upon which Jesus was executed. This was a common form of capital punishment.

crown of thorns: The Roman soldiers attempted to mock Jesus for His claim of kingship by forcing Him to wear a crown made of sharp thorns.

crucifixion: The method used by the Roman soldiers to put Christ to death. (See Matthew 27.)

Damascus road: Road on which Saul (later named Paul) was walking when he was converted to Christ. (See Acts 9:1–9.)

Daniel: Prophet during the reign of Nebuchadnezzar and Cyrus, he was noted for his trust in God. (See Daniel 1–2.)

David: One of the greatest kings of Israel, he united the tribes of Israel and began preparations for the temple. (See 1 Samuel 16.)

Davidic Covenant: God's promise that David would have a son who would build the temple, that David's house would forever rule, and that the Messiah (Jesus) would be one of David's descendants. (See 2 Samuel 7:12–16).

Day of the Lord: A time of intervention by God, for judgment or blessing.

deacon: A leader in the local church. Specific functions of deacons today vary among denominations.

Deborah: Judge of Israel who helped rescue her people. (See Judges 4:4–5.)

Decalogue: The Ten Commandments.

deism: A nonbiblical belief in God that states that God set the world in motion but does not really have anything to do with it on a day-to-day basis.

devil: One of the names for Satan, the fallen angel whose goal is to dethrone God and take over.

Dorcas: A woman in the New Testament days who did many good things for others. She was raised from the dead by Peter. (See Acts 9:36–42.)

Eden, Garden of: The first residence of humankind. It may have been somewhere near the Tigris and Euphrates Rivers. (See Genesis 2:15.)

Elijah: One of God's great Old Testament prophets. He departed from this world in a chariot of fire. (See 1 Kings 17 and 2 Kings 2.)

Elisha: The successor to Elijah, he was a prophet for more than half a century. (See 2 Kings 2–6.)

Elizabeth: Mother of John the Baptist. (See Luke 1:5–57.)

Emmanuel (Immanuel): A name given to Jesus meaning "God with us." (See Isaiah 7:14 and Matthew 1:22–23.)

empty tomb: Jesus' tomb, which He occupied from Good Friday evening until Sunday morning, when it was found empty—evidence of His resurrection (Matthew 28).

Enoch: An ancestor of Jesus, he did not die but instead was taken directly into heaven. (See Genesis 5:24.)

eschatology: The study of the events to happen at the end of the world.

Fall: The sin of Adam and Eve in the Garden of Eden,

which caused humankind to fall from out of fellow-ship with God. (See Genesis 3.)

fasting: The practice of not eating so as to consecrate yourself to prayer. It is an option and not a command for the Christian, and if done, should be done secretly to avoid pride. (See Matthew 6:16–18 and Acts 13:2–3.)

fishers of men: A term Jesus used to describe believ-ers who try to lead others to Him. (See Matthew 4:19.)

Flood: Early in the history of mankind, God saw so much wickedness in the world that He decided to start over again. Except for Noah and his family, the entire population was killed by the Flood. (See Gen-esis 6–9.)

Gethsemane: The garden where Jesus spent His last night before He was arrested. (See Matthew 26:36–56.)

Gideon: A judge of Israel. His story of courage in the face of danger from the advancing Midianites is one of the great Old Testament proofs of God's interven-tion to protect His own. (See Judges 6–8.)

gold, frankincense, myrrh: The precious gifts brought to the child Jesus by the Magi from the East. (See Luke 2.)

golden calf: An idol constructed by the children of Is-rael while Moses was on Mount Sinai meeting with God. (See Exodus 32.)

Golden Rule: "Do unto others as you would have them do to you." (See Luke 6:31.)

Goliath: The Philistine giant whom David killed with a sling. (See 1 Samuel 17:4–54.)

Good Friday: The day Jesus was crucified.

gospel: The message that Jesus Christ died on the

cross and rose again from the dead to forgive us the penalty of our sins.

Gospels: The first four books of the New Testament: Matthew, Mark, Luke, and John.

grace: God's act of giving us salvation and eternal life even though we do not deserve it.

Great Commission: Jesus' command to "go and make disciples of all nations, baptizing them in the name of the Father and of the Son and of the Holy Spirit." (See Matthew 28:19.)

Great Tribulation: A period of great trouble that will come on the earth, as foretold in the book of Revelation. (See Revelation 6.)

Great White Throne: A throne with Christ seated on it. At this throne, a time of judgment will be held for all who have never put faith in Jesus as Savior. This judgment will occur on earth at the end of time as we know it.

Hannah: Faithful woman of the Old Testament. She prayed for a son, and when God answered her prayer, she gave her son back to God to serve Him. (See 1 Samuel 1:1.)

handwriting on the wall: An incident in the time of Belshazzar, the king of Babylon. The writing was interpreted by Daniel. (See Daniel 5.)

heaven: The place where God the Father resides, along with the angels and the risen Jesus. It is the future home of all believers. (See Matthew 5:12 and Ephesians 6:9.)

hell: The place of punishment for all those who are unredeemed. (See Matthew 18:8–9.)

Herod the Great: King of Judea when Christ was born. (See Matthew 2:1–22.)

Holy Land: The geographic location of the events of

Jesus' day. It includes Israel and surrounding lands.
Holy of Holies: A special room that the Israelites in
the desert built in their tabernacle. Here the priest
would experience the presence of God's Spirit.
I AM: The name by which God revealed Himself to
Moses, indicating His faithfulness and eternity.
Also, I AM THAT I AM. (See Exodus 3:14.) Jesus
used the phrase to describe Himself in John 8:58.
"I am the way and the truth and the life": Jesus described Himself this way, emphasizing that He is the
only way to God. (See John 14:6.)
inerrancy: The belief that God's Word is absolutely
true and without error.
inspiration: Literally meaning "breathed into," it describes the method by which God communicated the
Bible to its human writers. (See 2 Timothy 3:16.)
Isaac: Son of Abraham and Sarah. He was born
when they were both well beyond their child-bearing
years. (See Genesis 21–25.)
Isaiah: Prophet of God who foretold the coming of
Jesus. (See Isaiah 9:6.)
Jacob: Son of Isaac and father of the twelve men who
would become the leaders of the twelve tribes of Israel. (See Genesis 25–50.)
Jairus' daughter: A child whom Jesus raised from
the dead. (See Luke 8:40–56.)
Jehovah: A name for God that comes from the Hebrew word YHWH. The Jews had so much respect for
God that they would not attempt to pronounce that
name. In many modern versions of the Old Testa-
ment it is translated as Lord.
Jerusalem: Capital of the southern kingdom, Judah.
Joseph (son of Jacob): Most beloved son of Jacob, he
was sold into slavery by his jealous brothers. Even-

tually he became second in command in Egypt, eventually to help his own family escape starvation by providing them with food. (See Genesis 37–50.)

Joseph (husband of Mary): Wanted to separate from Mary after he found out she was pregnant before they were married, but a visiting angel revealed to him that he should stay with her because the baby, Jesus, was conceived by the Holy Spirit. (See Matthew 1:16–24.)

Judas Iscariot: The disciple who betrayed Jesus. (See Matthew 26:47–56).

justification: This takes place at salvation, and it means that God declares the sinner righteous because of His faith in Jesus (Romans 3:24–28).

Lamb's Book of Life: The book in which God records the names of all those who have been saved. (see Revelation 13:8).

Last Supper: The meal shared by the disciples and Jesus on the night Jesus was betrayed. (see Matthew 26:14–16; 47–56.)

Law of Moses: The commands given by God to Moses, including the Ten Commandments, ceremonial and dietary laws, and myriad tenets spelled out in the biblical books of Exodus, Leviticus, and Deuteronomy.

Lazarus: A friend of Jesus whom Jesus raised from the dead. (See John 11.)

Lord's Day: Sunday. It became a special day because it was the day of Jesus' resurrection. Also, it was the day of the week on which the church was founded at Pentecost.

Lord's Prayer: The prayer Jesus gave to His disciples when they wanted to know how to pray. (See Matthew 6:9–13.)

"Mene, mene, tekel, parsin": The words that were written on the wall as a warning to King Belshazzar. (See Daniel 5.)

mercy: Holding back punishment from someone who has done wrong, which is what God did for us. As a Christian virtue, it extends to helping those who are down and out. (See James 2:1–13.)

mercy seat: The covering on the ark of the covenant that sat in the tabernacle of the Israelites.

Methuselah: The oldest man who ever lived. He was 969 years old when he died. (See Genesis 5:27.)

miracles: Extraordinary events that can be explained only by a supernatural cause.

Moses: The man God used to lead the Israelites out of captivity in Egypt and into a position to enter the land He had promised them.

Mount Ararat: The mountain on which Noah's ark came to rest after the Flood. (See Genesis 8:4.)

Mount Carmel: The site of Elijah's great showdown with the prophets of Baal. God performed a miracle there to prove His greatness. (See 1 Kings 18:16–46.)

Mount of Olives: A ridge east of Jerusalem, it was the site of the beginning of Jesus' triumphal entry into Jerusalem shortly before His death. (See Mark 11:1.)

Mount Sinai: The mountain where God met with, talked to, and gave the Law to Moses. (See Exodus 19.)

mustard seed: A tiny seed that Jesus used as a symbol of our faith. (See Matthew 17:20.)

Nazareth: Jesus' hometown. (See Luke 1:26–27.)

new birth: The spiritual process by which a lost sinner gains eternal life.

new heaven and new earth: A new world that will replace the "first earth" when it is destroyed. (See Revelation 21:1.)

new man, old man: Conflicting desires that war within every Christian. The old nature keeps trying to influence us to do evil. Even while we enjoy the good of the new nature (2 Peter 1:4), we have to be careful what the old nature does (Romans 7:18).

Nicodemus: A Pharisee who visited Jesus one night to learn from Jesus. Jesus told him he had to be born again. (See John 3:1–21.)

Ninevah: A city to which God sent the prophet Jonah, to warn the people to repent. (See the book of Jonah.)

Noah: The man God chose to preserve humankind by building an ark that would withstand the Flood God sent. (See Genesis 6.)

Palm Sunday: The Sunday before Easter. It commemorates the day Jesus rode triumphantly into Jerusalem and was hailed as king. (See Matthew 21.)

parables: Stories Jesus told to clarify a point or to bring a message to His listeners.

Passover: A Jewish feast day that commemorates death "passing over" the homes of obedient Israelites in Egypt. (See Exodus 12.)

Pentateuch: The first five books of the Old Testament.

Pentecost: A Jewish feast day that occurred fifty days after the Passover feast. It was also the day of the beginning of the church. (See Acts 2.)

Peter's denial: Not long after Peter promised Jesus he would never deny Him, he did just that—three times. (See Matthew 26:69–75.)

Prince of Peace: Another name given to Jesus by the prophet Isaiah. (See Isaiah 9:6.)

Prodigal Son: One of Jesus' most famous parables, it

told of a young man who ran away with his inherit-ance and blew it on riotous living. Amazingly, when he returned, broke and discouraged, his father wel-comed him with open arms. (See Luke 15:11–32.)

Rachel: The wife of Jacob and the mother of Joseph and Benjamin. (See Genesis 29–30.)

Rebecca: The wife of Isaac and the mother of Esau and Jacob. (See Genesis 24.).

Red Sea: The body of water that stood between the Israelites and freedom from the pursuing Egyptians. God parted the sea miraculously, allowing the Isra-elites to escape. (See Exodus 13:17–14:31.)

Resurrection: The coming back to life of Jesus Christ. The apostle Paul wrote that without the truth of the Resurrection, our faith is in vain. (See 1 Corin-thians 15:12–29.)

Sabbath: The seventh day of the week, set aside by Jewish law for rest and worship, following the exam-ple God set at Creation, and the Ten Command-ments. After the church began to function, Christians began to set aside the first day, Sunday, instead of Saturday, the Sabbath.

salvation: The gift of God that is given to all who put their faith in what He did for us through Jesus' death on the cross. Only through this salvation can we be rescued from a sure future of separation from God. (See Acts 4:12 and Ephesians 2:13–18.)

sanctification: The state of being set apart from the world to grow more and more like Christ.

Sarah: The wife of Abraham and the mother of Isaac. (See Genesis 15:17–27.)

Sea of Galilee: The body of water around which much of the ministry of Jesus took place. It is where Jesus walked on water.

Second Coming: Jesus' promised return. We do not know when He is returning, but it could be at any time. (See John 14:3, Luke 12:40, and Acts 1:11.).

Sermon on the Mount: A message Jesus gave as He stood near the Sea of Galilee. The sermon gives us Jesus' guidelines for living in a way that pleases Him. (See Matthew 5–7.)

serpent: The form that Satan took when he tempted Adam and Eve in the Garden of Eden. (See Genesis 3.)

seven last words of Christ: As Jesus hung dying on the cross, He uttered seven sentences: "Father, forgive them for they do not know what they are doing" (Luke 23:34). "I tell you the truth, today you will be with me in paradise" (v. 43). "Dear woman, here is your son" (John 19:26). "My God, my God, why have You forsaken me?" (Matthew 27:46). "I thirst" (John 19:28). "It is finished" (John 19:30). "Father, into your hands I commit my spirit" (Luke 23:46).

sin: Anything in us that runs counter to God's character or misses the mark of what God expects of us. He is completely holy and cannot tolerate unholiness. Therefore we must have His forgiveness for our sins before we can enter His heaven.

Sodom and Gomorrah: Two cities that were destroyed by God because of the wickedness there. (See Genesis 19.)

Solomon: Perhaps the wisest man who ever lived, Solomon was the son of King David and the author of Proverbs, Ecclesiastes, and Song of Solomon.

sovereignty of God: The doctrine that says God is supreme. He answers to no one and all of His decisions and actions are right.

Stephen: The first Christian martyr, who was stoned

to death for preaching the gospel. (See Acts 7:54–60.)

tabernacle: The portable worship center that the people of Israel constructed under God's direction. (See Exodus 25–29.)

temple: The permanent worship center used by the Israelites throughout the Old Testament era. Solomon built the first one. (See 2 Samuel 7 and 1 Chronicles 17.)

Ten Commandments: The Law of God, given to Moses on Mount Sinai. (See Exodus 19–20.)

Transfiguration: The visible transformation of Jesus demonstrating His glory as the Son of God. (See Matthew 17:1–8.)

upper room: The place where Jesus and His disciples enjoyed the Last Supper and Jesus identified Judas as His betrayer. (See Luke 22.)

Virgin Birth: The truth that Jesus Christ came into the world through a human mother but had no human father at conception. He was conceived miraculously through the Holy Spirit and so did not inherit the sinful nature that afflicts all other humans born of both man and woman. (See Matthew 1:18–25.)

Virgin Mary: The mother of Jesus. She was chosen by God to conceive His Son, which she did before she ever had sexual intercourse. She later had other children through natural means.

worship: The act of adoring, praising, and glorifying God. As the created, we worship the Creator. As the redeemed, we worship the Redeemer.

Zacchaeus: A tax collector whose life was changed when He climbed a tree to see Jesus. (See Luke 19:1–10.)

This is the kind of list you go back to often as you build on your knowledge of God's Word, using it as a checklist to see how much you know, or how much you need to know. But the list is by no means exhaustive. We will never run out of things that we can learn from our study of Scripture. Do not be discouraged if you begin to think there is far too much to learn. No one—not even the greatest biblical scholar—can fully grasp all there is to know about God. We can, however, build on the basics and create a solid foundation, all with the knowledge that one day when we see our Lord face-to-face He will provide us with everything He wants us to know. Until then, our task is to learn all we can and apply what we know so we can serve our God.

Appendix B

Scriptures That Speak to Your Needs

When you need to know more about God
Yours, O Lord, is the greatness and the power and the glory and the majesty and the splendor, for everything in heaven and earth is yours. Yours, O Lord, is the kingdom; you are exalted as head over all (1 Chronicles 29:11).

You are a forgiving God, gracious and compassionate, slow to anger and abounding in love (Nehemiah 9:17).

For this God is our God for ever and ever; he will be our guide even to the end (Psalm 48:14).

You are forgiving and good, O Lord, abounding in love to all who call to you (Psalm 86:5).

I will sing of the Lord's great love forever; with my mouth I will make your faithfulness known to all generations (Psalm 89:1).

The Lord reigns, he is robed in majesty; the Lord is robed in majesty and is armed with strength. The world is firmly established, it cannot be moved (Psalm 93:1).

Your throne was established long ago; you are from all eternity
(Psalm 93:2).

The Lord is compassionate and gracious, slow to anger, abounding in love (Psalm 103:8).

The Lord is good to all; he has compassion on all he has made (Psalm145:9).

Ah, Sovereign Lord, you have made the heavens and the earth by your great power and outstretched arm. Nothing is too hard for you (Jeremiah 32:17).

The Lord is good, a refuge in times of trouble. He cares for those who trust in him (Nahum 1:7).

Who shall separate us from the love of Christ? Shall trouble or hardship or persecution or famine or nakedness or danger or sword? . . . No, in all these things we are more than conquerors through him who loved us (Romans 8:35, 37).

Oh, the depth of the riches of the wisdom and knowledge of God! How unsearchable his judgments and his paths beyond tracing out! (Romans 11:33).

But He said to me, "My grace is sufficient for you, for my power is made perfect in weakness." Therefore I will boast all the more gladly about my weaknesses, so that Christ's power may rest on me (2 Corinthians 12:9).

If we confess our sins, he is faithful and just and will forgive us our sins and purify us from all unrighteousness (1 John1:9).

When you need comfort

The Lord is my shepherd, I shall not be in want. He makes me lie down in green pastures, he leads me beside quiet waters, he restores my soul. He guides me in paths of righteousness for his name's sake. Even though I walk through the valley of the shadow of death, I will fear no evil, for you are with me: your rod and your staff, they comfort me. You prepare a table before me in the presence of my enemies. You anoint my head with oil; my cup overflows. Surely goodness and love will follow me all the days of my life, and I will dwell in the house of the Lord forever (Psalm 23).

As a father has compassion on his children, So the Lord has compassion on those who fear him (Psalm 103:13).

For he knows how we are formed, he remembers that we are dust (Psalm 103:14).

Blessed are those who mourn, for they will be comforted (Matthew 5:4).

I have told you these things, so that in me you may have peace. In this world you will have trouble. But take heart! I have overcome the world (John 16:33).

And we know that in all things God works for the good of those who love him, who have been called according to his purpose (Romans 8:28).

May our Lord Jesus Christ himself and God our Father, who loved us and by His grace gave us eternal encouragement and good hope, encourage your hearts and strengthen you in every good deed and word (2 Thessalonians 2:16–17).

When you need to find:
The Ten Commandments
Exodus 20:1–17

A description of the tabernacle in the wilderness
Exodus 25–31

The Golden Rule
Matthew 7:12

Jesus' birth
Matthew 1–2
Luke 1–2

The Lord's Prayer
Matthew 6:9–13

The Beatitudes
Matthew 5:3–10

Jesus' most noteworthy miracles:
Turning water into wine John 2

Walking on the water—Matthew 14:22–33; Mark 6:47–51; John 6:16–24
Feeding the five thousand—Matthew 14:13–21; Mark 6:32–44; Luke 9:10–17; John 6:1–14
Raising Lazarus from the dead—John 11:1–44
Paying taxes from a coin in a fish—Matthew 17:24–27
The great fish catch—John 21:1–14

Jesus' great prayer to God
John 17

Jesus' words from the cross
"Father, forgive them, for they do not know what they are doing" (Luke 23:34).
"I tell you the truth, today you will be with me in paradise" (Luke 23:43).
To Mary: "Dear woman, here is your son." To John: "Here is your mother" (John 19:26–27).
"My God, my God, why have you forsaken me?" (Matthew 27:46).
"I am thirsty" (John 19:28).
"It is finished" (John 19:30).
"Father, into your hands I commit my spirit" (Luke 23:46).

The Great Commission
Matthew 28:19–20

The Love Chapter
1 Corinthians 13

The fruit of the Spirit
Galatians 5:22–23

The armor of God
Ephesians 6:10–17

The faith hall of fame
Hebrews 11

Note to the Reader

The publisher invites you to share your response to the message of this book by writing Discovery House Publishers, P. O. Box 3566, Grand
Rapids, MI 49501, U.S.A. or by calling 1–800–653–
8333. For information about other Discovery House
publications, contact us at the same address and
phone number.